NATIONAL
GEOGRAPHIC
KiDS

ULTIMATE
Explorer
FIELD GUIDE

Birds

Julie Beer

NATIONAL GEOGRAPHIC
WASHINGTON, D.C.

Contents

MONK PARAKEET p. 87

BLUE JAY p. 96

GREAT HORNED OWL p. 70

LET'S GO Birding!

BIRDING IS LIKE A TREASURE HUNT. Every time you go outside—whether it's into your backyard or into a national park—you can discover a winged wonder. Ask yourself: What's out there today? What will I find? Then look into the sky to see a tiny Chimney Swift somersaulting through the air to catch an insect dinner. Look down to see a Killdeer dragging its wing across the ground as if it's broken, to draw enemies away from its nest. Look into the trees to discover a nest filled with robin babies' open beaks, waiting for their mom to return with food. Look across a lake or marsh to see a Great Blue Heron flapping its massive wings in flight, like an ancient flying dinosaur. Why do we love to watch birds? Of all the animals in nature, birds are the easiest to find and enjoy. About 10,000 species have been named around the world, and more than 900 of those species live in North America. They bring excitement and joy to more than 44 million Americans each year. Join them! You can get started right now on a tour of the 175 bird species in this book that live across the nation. You'll find all kinds—from tiny, jewel-colored hummingbirds to huge predators like the majestic Bald Eagle. The birds appear in their taxonomic order—the way they are ranked by family in the animal kingdom. A good way to see birds quickly is to put out a bird feeder. Soon you'll be identifying its visitors. As you locate each bird in this book, be sure to keep a list, and add to it throughout the year. Soon you'll call yourself a birder. Welcome to the club!

— The Editors

HOW TO USE This Book

GET OUTSIDE! LOOK AROUND! Take this book with you! Use the many special features of this field guide to discover how to spot birds and pick up expert tips.

Bird Entry

THIS IS WHERE YOU'LL FIND THE BIRD'S COMMON NAME.

THE RANGE MAP SHOWS WHERE THE SPECIES CAN BE FOUND. THE COLOR-CODED KEY GIVES THE TIMES OF YEAR THE BIRD IS IN AN AREA IN NORTH AMERICA.

HERE IS THE BIRD'S SCIENTIFIC NAME, ITS AVERAGE LENGTH, THE HABITAT IT LIVES IN, THE FOOD IT EATS, AND THE SOUNDS IT MAKES.

THIS TEXT GIVES YOU A GENERAL DESCRIPTION OF THE SPECIES, INCLUDING KEY BEHAVIORS, HUNTING AND EATING HABITS, AND SOME SURPRISING FACTS.

BIRD JOKES AND RIDDLES WILL MAKE YOU AND YOUR FRIENDS LAUGH.

USE THESE DESCRIPTIVE LABELS TO QUICKLY IDENTIFY A BIRD. CAN YOU NAME IT IN TEN SECONDS?

DISCOVER AN INTERESTING BIRD BEHAVIOR SPECIFIC TO THIS SPECIES.

[Sample Bird Entry]

BALD EAGLE

Haliaeetus leucocephalus LENGTH 34 in (86 cm) HABITAT: Lakes, rivers, marshes, swamps, seacoasts FOOD: Fish, reptiles, small mammals, birds VOICE: A twittering *kwit-kwit-kwit-kee-kee-kee-kee*

WE ALL KNOW the Bald Eagle as the majestic emblem of the United States, but in the early days of the nation, not everyone was a fan of this impressive bird. Benjamin Franklin believed it was a bird of "bad moral character" because it often steals food from other birds. (Franklin thought the Wild Turkey was a better candidate.) The Bald Eagle prefers fish as food, although it will also hunt small animals like reptiles, frogs, birds, and shellfish. This eagle isn't bald. The term is an old-fashioned way of referring to the white feathers of an adult eagle's head, which contrast with its brown body and wings. Usually found near water, Bald Eagles build huge stick nests high in trees, often piling more sticks on top of a previous year's nest. One nest in Ohio weighed more than 2 tons (1.8 MT)—as much as a small car! It didn't topple the tree because these eagles choose large trees and construct their nests around thick trunks and stout limb forks.

Laugh Out Loud!
What kind of bird doesn't need a comb?

→ LOOK FOR THIS
If you spot a **BALD EAGLE** going another bird a rough time, it isn't pulling its rank on our national bird. Instead, it may be trying to steal the other bird's hard-earned catch. Bald Eagles often forget (egress and steal fresh-caught fish right from their talons. In general, the Bald Eagle doesn't spend much of its time on a search for food. In winter, it tends to chill in the chill, spending up to 98 percent of the time perched in a tree—perhaps wishing that Ospreys made deliveries?

BILL WITH HOOKED TIP

ADULT

LARGE SHARP TALONS

38 HAWKS, KITES, EAGLES, AND ALLIES (ACCIPITRIDAE)

Range Map

>>> RANGE MAP

BREEDING
YEAR-ROUND
MIGRATION
WINTER

THE MAP   THE KEY

THE RANGE MAP for each bird species shows where the bird can be found in North America. The color-coded key explains the bird's range during certain times of the year: breeding season, migration, and winter. Some species stay in the same location year-round.

SPECIAL FEATURES called Birdtastics give you a closer look at unique bird habitats, strange bird behaviors, birds that are now extinct, and more.

A CAPTION DESCRIBES THE MAIN PHOTO.

A TEXT BLOCK GIVES GENERAL INFORMATION ABOUT THE FEATURED HABITAT, BEHAVIOR, OR SPECIES.

DISCOVER HABITATS LIKE THE OPEN OCEAN AND FIND OUT WHAT KINDS OF BIRDS LIVE THERE.

Classification

BIRD SPECIES ARE GROUPED TOGETHER IN FAMILIES—

based on their physical characteristics and genetic makeup. This classification is called taxonomy, and scientific family names are written in Latin. Birds in this book are arranged by the families they belong in. The common family names, along with the scientific ones, can be found at the bottom of the pages.

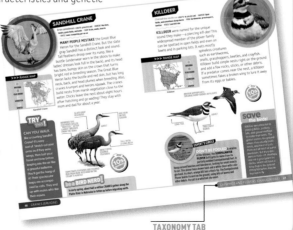

TAXONOMY TAB

GETTING STARTED:
Field Tricks & Tips

IF YOU LIKE TO LOOK AT BIRDS, read more about them, and identify species, then you're ready to be a birder! Here are a few things you can do to get started.

Where to Find Them

Birds are everywhere. That's the great thing about being a birder—you can walk right out the front door and start looking! You'll soon find that specific kinds, or species, of birds live in specific habitats—the climate, landscape, and plant life of a place. For instance, you'll see a Roadrunner in the deserts of the Southwest and Snowy Owls in the Arctic tundra. That's because those places offer what those specific birds need to survive: food, protection from predators, and a safe spot for nesting. So when you go looking for a bird, first think about the habitat you might find it in. A Barn Owl lives in—you guessed it!—a barn and other big buildings where it can make a nest and be close to open fields that have plenty of mice and other small mammals for food. So if you're around a farm, take a look for a Barn Owl. Some birds aren't particularly easy to spot, but if you know the habitat they live in you can be on alert!

Each bird entry in this book describes the bird's habitat. It also gives a map showing the range—or area—they live in. Some stay in one place all year round. Others

migrate, or fly to different places at different times of the year, so their range is wide and their type of habitat can vary.

What They Look Like

Birders need to pay attention to details! Whether you're watching a bird sitting on a fence outside your window or you're looking through a pair of binoculars at a bird in flight, know what to look for. A bird's "field marks" tell you something unique about the bird that will help you identify it. Here are the most important things to look for when trying to identify a bird:

- ✓ Color
- ✓ Color patterns
- ✓ Size
- ✓ Shape
- ✓ Behavior
- ✓ Song
- ✓ Habitat
- ✓ Geographical range

Identifying just two or three of these items will help you significantly narrow down a bird species. Sometimes the only difference between two species is a slight variation in a marking. For that reason, it's good to have your field guide handy when you're out looking for birds. Also, be sure to take a mental picture of a bird you spot. Try to remember as many details as possible

Baltimore Oriole

and write them in a notebook so you can recognize that bird in the future.

Here's an important thing to know about bird identification: Males and females of the same species can look very different. Males often have the more colorful feathers! So it's good to know what the male and female of a particular species look like. To make matters even more challenging, some birds have different color patterns during different times of year. During certain times, birds go through a process called molting, when they lose old feathers and grow new ones—and the timing is different for different birds. No one said birding was going to be simple!

What to Listen For

Songs and notes are another clue to help you identify a bird. Bird species have a unique song or call, which can be a sure giveaway for identifying that species. Sometimes you'll hear a song first, like a Mourning Dove's *oowoo-woo-woo-woo*, and then you can follow the song to the bird.

Be a Bird Lover

When you spend time watching birds, you quickly gain respect for how beautiful, powerful, smart, and graceful they are. They're also sensitive. Here are a few things you need to know:

Outdoor cats that prey on birds and their nests have driven down bird populations in some areas. To help protect birds, keep cats indoors.

Birds are very sensitive to pollutants and pesticides. Talk to your parents about avoiding the use of chemicals to control pests in your yard or garden. Insects are important food for birds!

Birds can be injured or killed when they become entangled in plastic bags and plastic packaging. Before recycling or discarding plastic bags, tie them in a knot. Cut open plastic soda rings so a bird's head can't get stuck in it.

Winter can be a tough time of year for our feathered friends when it comes to finding food. Put up bird feeders in the winter to help out birds that are in your yard year-round. Keep the feeders clean and make sure to hang them in a spot that squirrels and cats can't reach.

✓ **CHECKLIST FOR BIRDERS**
Want to be a pro bird-watcher? Here's a checklist to get you started.

✓ **BRING BINOCS**
A good pair of binoculars is a must for birding. First use your naked eye to scan for birds, and then bring the binoculars up for a closer view. It's hard to scan an area through the magnified lenses.

✓ **GET A GOOD GUIDE**
Be sure to bring this book on your hikes or car trips. But since there are fewer than 200 birds in this book and hundreds more in the wild, you might also want to use the *National Geographic Backyard Guide to the Birds of North America* or the *National Geographic Field Guide to the Birds of North America*. And check out the app based on this guide. Both will help you identify nearly 1,000 species!

✓ **MAKE A NOTE OF IT**
Grab a small spiral notebook and a pen or pencil for your backpack. You'll find out more about the importance of taking notes on page 13.

✓ **GO CAMO**
Dress in camouflage colors—neutral tones like tans and dark greens—so you'll look like part of a grassy, bushy, or tree-lined landscape. Bright colors can scare away birds. Wear a hat for sun protection, but avoid wearing sunglasses—they make it harder to spot birds. Why? Birds are camouflaged, too!

Timing Is Everything

To spot a specific bird species, you have to time it just right. Songbirds, for instance, have a very predictable pattern: They are lively before dawn in the spring and summer. They wake up hungry and spend their morning eating. When it's hot in the summer and cold in the winter, they often retreat during the afternoon and don't reappear until after sunset. You know what this means: The early bird gets the worm when it comes to looking for songbirds! To spot an owl in flight, you're likely going to have to wait until night, although you might get lucky and spot one roosting during the day.

Shh!

Birds startle very easily. Be quiet and keep your distance so they don't fly away before you've had a chance to get a good look.

Watch Your Step

If you're in a marshy area or at the beach where birds might be nesting on the ground, be careful where you step. And don't disturb a nest if you come across one. If you happen upon a baby bird on the ground, resist the temptation to pick it up. Chances are the mother will be back soon and will tend to it. If you're in doubt about what to do with a bird out of the nest, call your local Audubon Society or a veterinarian.

Take Notes!

Birding is very hands-on. When you're not looking through binoculars and checking your field guide, you should jot down a few observations you made. Keep a list of birds you spotted—or think you've spotted—and then when you go home you can do more research. It's fun to keep a collective list

of all the species you've identified. You can also use a notebook or sketch pad to draw a picture of the birds you see. This helps you remember all those details about markings.

Bring the Birds to You

Don't want to travel the world to go birding? Try turning your backyard into a bird-friendly habitat. You'll attract certain birds depending on the kind of plants you grow. A yard with tall trees can attract tanagers and orioles. A yard with shrubs can lure in Song Sparrows. Even a wide-open, manicured lawn can attract birds—like American Robins and European Starlings. Birds also need a reliable water source. Birdbaths with fresh water will attract all kinds of species—even some that aren't attracted to bird feeders.

You can also invite birds to your yard by building a nest box—also known as a birdhouse. The kind of box you build is specific for each species. Search for "nest boxes" on the website for the Cornell Lab of Ornithology: allaboutbirds.org. You'll find the right design to welcome your backyard birds.

Turn the page to get started finding and identifying birds!

CANADA GOOSE

Branta canadensis LENGTH 40 in (102 cm) ▪ HABITAT Ponds, suburbs, parks ▪ FOOD Grass, grains ▪ VOICE A deep *honk-a-lonk* call

IT'S EASY TO UNDERSTAND why Canada Geese earned the nickname "honker." Their deep, nasal call can be heard across the ponds and open spaces where they live. Canada Geese eat grasses, grains, and berries and can weigh up to 20 pounds (9 kg). The oldest known wild Canada Goose lived to be 30! Canada Geese mate for life and stay together throughout the year. In fall, some migrate from Canada to warmer parts of North America, flying day and night in a V formation. If the wind is good, they can cover 1,500 miles (2,400 km) in just 24 hours! Watch for them in flight: See their brown wings and blackish lower back and tail. A white rump band is a sure sign it's a Canada Goose.

be a BIRD NERD!

CANADA GEESE can be real pests. They like to hang out on the manicured lawns of city parks, golf courses, and airports. Besides being a hazard for planes, they are also a pain for golfers, who have to be careful where they step—50 Canada Geese produce 2.5 tons (2.3 MT) of droppings a year! Canada Geese populations have exploded since the 1940s: Some five million live in North America.

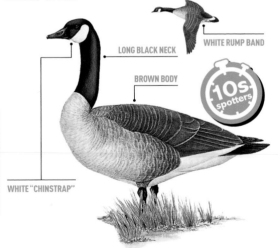

WHITE RUMP BAND

LONG BLACK NECK

BROWN BODY

WHITE "CHINSTRAP"

10s spotters

>>> RANGE MAP

- BREEDING
- YEAR-ROUND
- MIGRATION
- WINTER

Laugh Out Loud!

What is a Canada Goose's favorite type of TV show?

Duck-u-mentaries!

WOOD DUCK

Aix sponsa LENGTH 18.5 in (47 cm) • HABITAT Swamps, marshes • FOOD Plants, grasses, berries, grain • VOICE Females: a high-pitched *ooo-eeek-ooo-eeek!;* males: a rising and falling whistle, *zeeet!*

MALE WOOD DUCKS are known for their striking colors—almost every one of their feathers has a delicate pattern on it. This duck gets its name from its habitat—wooded swamps and streams. Wood ducks are one of the few kinds of ducks that nest in holes in trees and have claws to grip branches. They mostly eat grasses, seeds, and fruits.

>>> RANGE MAP

BREEDING

YEAR-ROUND

WINTER

BUSHY CREST MAKES HEAD APPEAR LARGE AND ROUNDED

10s spotters

UNIQUE PATTERN; MALE'S COLORS GLISTEN BLUE AND GREEN IN GOOD LIGHT

→ **LOOK FOR THIS** Identify a Wood Duck in water: **WATCH ITS HEAD.** When it swims, its head bobs back and forth like a pigeon's!

NORTHERN PINTAIL

Anas acuta LENGTH 20–26 in (51–66 cm) • HABITAT Marshes, open areas with ponds • FOOD Grains, seeds, plants, insects • VOICE Males: a whistled call; females: a single quack or series of quacks

THE LONG-NECKED NORTHERN PINTAIL can be found in ponds, wetlands, and marshes, especially in the West. It has two long tail feathers that extend far past its other feathers, and is sometimes called a "sharp-tailed duck." Northern Pintails are early spring nesters, starting as soon as the ice melts in the North. They build their nests on the ground near grasses and bushes.

10s spotters

MALE: WHITE CHEST AND STRIPE UP THE NECK

FEMALE

MALE: LONG TAIL

>>> RANGE MAP

BREEDING

YEAR-ROUND

MIGRATION

WINTER

MALLARD

Anas platyrhynchos **LENGTH** 23 in (58 cm) • **HABITAT** Ponds, parks, wetlands • **FOOD** Insect larvae, snails, seeds • **VOICE** Males make a raspy *kreep* call; females give a loud *quack!*

THE MALLARD is the most abundant duck in the world and the ancestor of almost all domestic ducks. More than 30 million Mallards live on the planet, and more than half of them live in North America. They are found around freshwater habitats—often in city parks and ponds. Mallards make their nests on the ground near the water and eat mostly insect larvae and snails—and handouts from park visitors. Strong fliers, Mallards can spring from the water straight into the air. They are also speedy—migrating flocks have been clocked at 55 miles an hour (88.5 km/h). After breeding season, Mallards lose all their flight feathers. They lay low for three or four weeks, waiting for their feathers to grow back.

>>> RANGE MAP

- ☐ BREEDING
- ☐ YEAR-ROUND
- ☐ MIGRATION
- ☐ WINTER

MAKE THIS!

Mallards are easy to draw. Break them down by shape.

BODY: Draw an oval for the body. Add a triangle tail at one end of the oval and two lines at the bottom of the oval for legs. Add a wing inside the oval.

HEAD: Draw a small circle for the head. Add a dot for the eye and a triangle for the beak.

NECK: Connect head and body with a rectangle for the neck.

FEET: Add two rectangles for feet!

THEN COLOR!

10s spotters

ORANGE BILL WITH DARK SADDLE

MOTTLED, OR SPECKLED, FEATHERS

YELLOW BILL

GREEN HEAD

FEMALE

CURLED TAIL FEATHERS

MALE

→ LOOK FOR THIS MALLARDS are known for tipping up—using the familiar "butt-in-the-air-and-head-underwater" position that allows them to pick food off the pond bottom.

RED-BREASTED MERGANSER

Mergus serrator LENGTH 25 in (64 cm) • HABITAT Lakes, rivers, oceans • FOOD Fish, mollusks, crustaceans • VOICE Usually silent; females: sometimes a harsh *kerr-kerr* sound

THESE ARE LARGE, LONG-BODIED, diving ducks. The male has an impressive shaggy crest on the back of its green head. The Red-breasted Merganser can be found near rivers, lakes, and oceans. It nests on the ground, often under a boulder or near shrubs, and dives underwater to catch its prey— mainly fish.

>>> RANGE MAP

- ☐ BREEDING
- ☐ YEAR-ROUND
- ☐ MIGRATION
- ☐ WINTER

MALE: LONG, THIN ORANGE BILL

SHAGGY DOUBLE CREST

WHITE COLLAR

RUDDY DUCK

Oxyura jamaicensis LENGTH 15 in (38 cm) • HABITAT Wetlands, marshes, ponds, tidal estuaries • FOOD Aquatic insects, zooplankton • VOICE Usually silent; males make belching sound during courtship

RUDDY DUCKS are known for their squatty neck and the male's distinctive aqua blue bill in spring and summer. Expert divers, they live near wetlands, marshes, and brackish bays. They often nest in cattails or grass. Ruddy Ducks find aquatic insects and crustaceans by diving to the bottom of shallow water, scooping up mud, and straining the juicy tidbits with their bills.

THICK NECK

MALE: WHITE CHEEKS

FEMALE

>>> RANGE MAP

- ☐ BREEDING
- ☐ YEAR-ROUND
- ☐ MIGRATION
- ☐ WINTER

GAMBEL'S QUAIL

Callipepla gambelii LENGTH 11 in (28 cm) • HABITAT Lowland desert washes; river valleys • FOOD Plants, seeds, berries • VOICE A loud *chi-CA-go-go* call; sometimes a *qua-el*

GAMBEL'S QUAIL has a plump, pear-shaped body and a feathered plume on top of its head. These sociable birds are found in the Desert Southwest and Great Basin. They roost in low trees at night and nest on the ground, sheltered by shrubs or prickly pear cactus. Gambel's Quail eat plants and seeds and, though they live in very dry areas, they require a lot of water. They travel along the ground in family groups called coveys that can include more than a dozen birds. If frightened, they scurry for cover. When they do fly, they take to the air with an explosive burst of energy over a short distance. Gambel's Quail are named after William Gambel, a 19th-century naturalist and explorer of the American Southwest.

save the birds!

Gambel's Quail visit backyards for birdseed and water. Unfortunately, house cats find this quail to be pretty tasty! Be sure to keep your cat indoors!

>>> RANGE MAP

YEAR-ROUND

→ LOOK FOR THIS

Male and female **GAMBEL'S QUAIL** have a comma-shaped top-knot of feathers on their heads that bobs forward as they scurry along. The male has a dark forehead, black throat, and black patch on its belly. The female has an unmarked white belly and a smaller topknot. Both have a chestnut crown and chestnut sides on their chunky bodies. When a predator approaches, they burst into noisy flight.

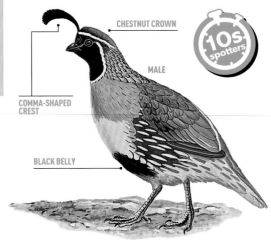

CHESTNUT CROWN

MALE

COMMA-SHAPED CREST

BLACK BELLY

10s spotters

NORTHERN BOBWHITE

Colinus virginianus LENGTH 9.75 in (25 cm) • HABITAT Grassy
fields, pine woods • FOOD Seeds, berries, plants, insects • VOICE Males
make the whistling *bob-WHITE* call

NAMED AFTER the male's distinctive
call—*bob-WHITE!*—the Northern Bob-
white is the only native quail in the East. A
plump, ground-dwelling bird with a short tail
and a slight crest, it is found in rural, agricultural areas away from
towns. It nests in fields
and dense underbrush and eats seeds, berries,
and insects. This quail scurries along the
ground in groups, bursting into flight when
startled. Then it finds cover and stands frozen
until it is safe. Luckily, its dappled feathers
make excellent camouflage.

>>> RANGE MAP

YEAR-ROUND

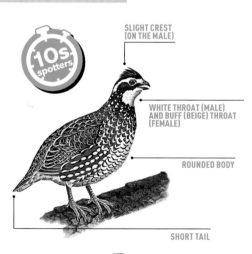

SLIGHT CREST
(ON THE MALE)

10s.
spotters

WHITE THROAT (MALE)
AND BUFF (BEIGE) THROAT
(FEMALE)

ROUNDED BODY

SHORT TAIL

save
the birds!

Northern Bobwhites
are disappearing. As
cities spread into the
countryside, there are
fewer grassy fields and
woods for them to call
home. Modern farms use
pesticides and herbicides
to kill the insects and
weeds that these quail
like to eat. One way you
can help is to volunteer
for organizations working
to save natural areas and
preserve farmland.

At night, NORTHERN BOBWHITES roost as a group on the ground. They keep a lookout for danger by
forming a circle with their tails facing the center and heads facing out.

WILD TURKEY

Meleagris gallopavo LENGTH Males: 46 in (117 cm); females: 37 in (94 cm) • HABITAT Open forests, fields • FOOD Seeds, nuts, berries • VOICE Male's gobble is a loud, shrill, descending call

THE TURKEYS we eat at Thanksgiving are the farm-raised version of the Wild Turkey that still struts around forests and fields in North America. The Wild Turkey has a distinctive red-and-blue bare head and a very large, plump body. Flocks search the ground looking for nuts, berries, and insects to eat. They make their nests under trees or in shrubs and roost in the trees at night. During courtship, males puff their feathers and flare their tails into a fan. Ben Franklin wanted the Wild Turkey to be the national bird of the United States, but Congress chose the Bald Eagle instead.

>>> RANGE MAP

YEAR-ROUND

be a BIRD NERD!

In the spring, a MALE'S GOBBLE can be heard a mile (1.6 km) away. In early spring, males gobble to tell hens, "I'm here." Hens make a yelp sound to let the male know their location. Both males and females cackle as they fly from their roosts. They also make purring calls as they strut around.

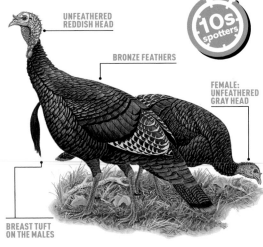

UNFEATHERED REDDISH HEAD

BRONZE FEATHERS

FEMALE: UNFEATHERED GRAY HEAD

10S spotters

BREAST TUFT ON THE MALES

What kind of key doesn't open any door?

A turkey!

RING-NECKED PHEASANT

Phasianus colchicus LENGTH 33 in (84 cm); females: 21 in (53 cm) · HABITAT Open country, farmland, woods · FOOD Seeds, grain, insects · VOICE Males crow like roosters throughout the day

ONE OF THE WORLD'S most popular game birds, the Ring-necked Pheasant was introduced to many parts of the world by the ancient Romans. Hunters recognize the *kak-CACK* sound it makes when it's surprised and suddenly flies, or flushes, from its cover. These birds nest in tall grasses and are most comfortable on the ground, eating seeds and insects.

>>> RANGE MAP

YEAR-ROUND

MALE: RED EYE PATCH
LONG, POINTED TAIL

WHITE NECK RING

FEMALE: BUFF-COLORED (BEIGE) OVERALL; SMALLER THAN THE MALE

RUFFED GROUSE

Bonasa umbellus LENGTH 17 in (43 cm) · HABITAT Forests, often along streams · FOOD Plants, fruit, acorns · VOICE Mostly quiet, males make a *queet* call when alarmed; females make a *pete-pete-peta-peta* call

THE RUFFED GROUSE gets its name from the black ruffs around its neck. This chicken-like bird lives in the forests of the northern United States and makes its nest in hollow stumps. The intestines of the Ruffed Grouse change in winter, allowing it to digest toxic buds of aspen trees. It also grows "snowshoes" that help it grip icy branches.

MALE HAS BLACK RUFF ON SIDES OF NECK

BANDED TAIL

>>> RANGE MAP

YEAR-ROUND

COMMON LOON

Gavia immer LENGTH 32 in (81 cm) ▪ HABITAT Northern lakes in the summer; coastal waters and ice-free lakes in winter ▪ FOOD Mostly fish ▪ VOICE Loud yodel call

A WATER BIRD that yodels? That's just loony. The Common Loon's distinctive call isn't the only thing that sets it apart: It also has eerie red eyes and huge webbed feet that can propel it more than 200 feet (61 m) below the water. When it catches a fish, it often swallows it underwater. The Common Loon spends summers nesting on lakes in Canada and the northern United States and winters in bays and harbors. Migrating loons sometimes mistake a wet parking lot or road for a lake. Once they've landed, they're often stranded because they can only take off from water—and they need up to a quarter mile (400 m) of open water as a runway.

>>> RANGE MAP

☐ BREEDING
☐ YEAR-ROUND
☐ MIGRATION
☐ WINTER

TRY THIS!

THE NEXT TIME you're at the swimming pool, try snorkeling like a Common Loon. Cover your eyes and have someone throw toys in the pool that are heavy enough to sink to the bottom. Then put on your goggles and a snorkel, if you have one, and cruise along the surface. When you spot a toy, take a big breath and dive like a loon to snatch it!

IN SUMMER THE COMMON LOON HAS A CHECKERBOARD BACK

DARK GREEN HEAD AND STRIPED COLLAR

WINTER BIRDS ARE MUCH PLAINER, WITH GRAYISH BROWN PLUMAGE

→ **LOOK FOR THIS** When on the lookout for fish, **COMMON LOONS** "snorkel"—swimming around the surface with their head underwater.

PIED-BILLED GREBE

Podilymbus podiceps LENGTH **13.5 in (34 cm)** • HABITAT **Marshy ponds and inlets** • FOOD **Fish, crustaceans, insects** • VOICE **Loud series of gulping notes—*kuk kuk kuk***

PIED-BILLED GREBES are little submarines, able to control their buoyancy by trapping water in their feathers. They catch fish and crustaceans by diving or slowly submerging. They can also float with their heads just above the surface. Rarely going on land, Pied-billed Grebes build floating nests in marshes, inlets, and wetlands. Their call can sound like gulping notes or chuckling chatter. Instead of webbed feet, grebes have lobed feet. Each toe has a large piece of skin that looks like a leaf. This helps them push quickly through the water. Grebes rarely fly.

>>> RANGE MAP

☐ BREEDING
☐ YEAR-ROUND
☐ WINTER

10S spotters

ADULT: BROWN OVERALL YEAR-ROUND

DOWNY YOUNG

BLACK RING AROUND BILL, BLACK CHIN, AND BLACK THROAT (DURING BREEDING SEASON)

save the birds!

Pied-billed Grebes are very secretive birds. They are rarely seen flying and are very good at disappearing in the thick bulrushes of the freshwater marshes where they live. If a Pied-billed Grebe needs to hide from an intruder, it slowly sinks in the water until only its head is showing—like a crocodile. When Pied-billed Grebes migrate, they travel at night.

be a BIRD NERD!

PIED-BILLED GREBES eat their own feathers. Sometimes feathers fill up half of their stomach. This prevents bones and other harmful parts of prey from passing into their intestines.

BIRDTASTICS:
Arctic Tundra Birds

Willow Ptarmigan

Lagopus lagopus

LENGTH: 15 in (38 cm)
EATS: Plants, insects
VOICE: Calls are growls, croaks, cackles

Snow Goose

Chen caerulescens

LENGTH: 30 in (76 cm)
EATS: Grass, grains
VOICE: Nasal honk call

Arctic Tern

Sterna paradisaea

LENGTH: 15.5 in (39 cm)
EATS: Fish, flying insects
VOICE: A *kee-errr* call
BE A BIRD NERD: It migrates from the Arctic to Antarctica, more than 25,000 miles (40,000 km)!

THE ARCTIC is the most northern part of the world, beginning at the North Pole and ending at the Arctic Circle. Summer temperatures rarely rise above 50 degrees F (10 degrees C). Trees don't grow in the cold, desertlike Arctic, but there is tundra—flat land where the ground thaws in summer. In May and June, millions of birds migrate here to nest.

WOOD STORK

Mycteria americana **LENGTH** 40 in (102 cm) • **HABITAT** Southern meadows, swamps, ponds, shallow coastal areas • **FOOD** Fish • **VOICE** Mostly silent; sometimes clack their bills

THE ONLY STORK that breeds in the United States, the Wood Stork feeds by touch as well as sight. It walks through shallow water, submerging its open bill. When a fish bumps it, the stork snaps its bill shut at lightning speed and eats the fish! With long legs, a featherless head, and a large bill, the Wood Stork is a real standout in a pond. Wood Storks are very social birds. They feed in flocks and nest in trees in large colonies called rookeries. In the hot summer, they regurgitate water and spray it over their chicks to keep them cool. You can't miss a Wood Stork in flight. Its wingspan can be 5.5 feet (1.7 m). That's the length of more than two tennis rackets.

>>> RANGE MAP

BREEDING

YEAR-ROUND

MIGRATION

save the birds!

Raccoons are one of the Wood Storks' biggest enemies. In dry years, they sneak across the shallow ponds and eat young storks or eggs in low nests. Biologists at the Harris Neck National Wildlife Refuge in Georgia solved that problem—they raised the water levels in their man-made ponds and filled them with alligators to eat the pesky raccoons. Suddenly, the raccoons stopped crossing the ponds and preying on the stork nests. Southern stork populations were on the endangered species list until 2014. Today, small populations of the birds are growing.

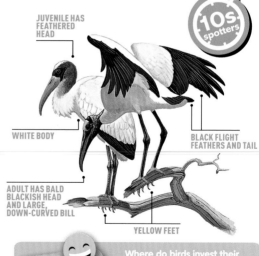

JUVENILE HAS FEATHERED HEAD

10S spotters

WHITE BODY

BLACK FLIGHT FEATHERS AND TAIL

ADULT HAS BALD BLACKISH HEAD AND LARGE, DOWN-CURVED BILL

YELLOW FEET

Laugh Out Loud!

Where do birds invest their money?

In the stork market!

DOUBLE-CRESTED CORMORANT

Phalacrocorax auritus LENGTH 32 in (81 cm)
• HABITAT Coasts, lakes, rivers • FOOD Fish • VOICE Usually silent, with some grunting noises

DOUBLE-CRESTED CORMORANTS are large, black, fish-eating birds with a small head and kinked neck. Living along coasts and near rivers and lakes, they are excellent divers, using their fully webbed feet to propel them underwater. They nest on rocks or cliffs and in trees in colonies with other cormorants and sometimes herons. The double crest is only visible on breeding adults and is usually white in cormorants breeding in the West and black in cormorants elsewhere.

>>> RANGE MAP

BREEDING

YEAR-ROUND

MIGRATION

WINTER

10s spotters

ORANGE AND YELLOW SKIN ON THE FACE

HOOKED BILL

KINKED NECK

JUVENILE IS DARK BROWN ABOVE AND HAS A PALE BREAST

ADULT HAS BLACK PLUMAGE (FEATHERS)

save the birds!

Birds like the Double-crested Cormorant can get injured or killed by getting their heads stuck in the plastic loops of soda can holders. These holders harm seabirds as well as land birds that hang out in junkyards, where trash ends up. Use scissors to cut open every ring before you recycle and throw the plastic away. It takes only a few seconds to help save a life!

→ **LOOK FOR THIS DOUBLE-CRESTED CORMORANTS** are often seen perched on piers or riverbanks with their wings spread wide, drying their feathers in the sun. Their feathers aren't waterproof like a duck's feathers. Instead, they become soaked and heavy when the bird dives in. The heaviness actually helps the cormorant dive deep to chase fish. When a cormorant swims, sometimes all you can see is its S-shaped neck and orange face. On land, cormorants are very clumsy walkers and use their hooked bills for balance.

AMERICAN WHITE PELICAN

Pelecanus erythrorhynchos **LENGTH 62 in (158 cm)**
- **HABITAT** Breeds on inland lakes; winters along the coast
- **FOOD** Fish • **VOICE** Mostly silent

AMERICAN WHITE PELICANS are superscoopers! Sometimes hunting in groups, they will herd fish into shallow water and then scoop them up with their bucket-like bill pouch. American White Pelicans do not plunge-dive to catch fish like the Brown Pelican—they "upend," or dunk their heads underwater with their tails skyward, like dabbling ducks. During breeding season, the male grows an unusual "horn" on the top of its bill. They nest in large colonies on inland lakes, building their nests on the ground and keeping eggs warm under their big webbed feet. With their large heads and huge bills, American White Pelicans look almost prehistoric. They are among the heaviest flying birds in the world.

>>> RANGE MAP

BREEDING
YEAR-ROUND
MIGRATION
WINTER

be a BIRD NERD!

Contrary to popular belief, this pelican never flies with fish in its pouch. It scoops up fish and swallows them before taking flight. This big bird tips the scales at a hefty 20 pounds (9 kg). Keep an eye on a pelican long enough and you'll probably see it try to snatch fish from another bird—even another pelican! It's successful about one-third of the time. Pelicans overheat in hot weather. Unlike humans, who can sweat, pelicans cool down by facing away from the sun, opening their bill, and fluttering their bill pouch.

DURING BREEDING SEASON, ADULTS GROW A "HORN" NEAR THE TIP OF THEIR BILL

10s spotters

WHITE WITH BLACK FEATHERS LINING THEIR BROAD WINGS

LARGE BRIGHT ORANGE BILL

Laugh Out Loud!

What kind of can doesn't need a can opener?

A PELI-can!

BROWN PELICAN

Pelecanus occidentalis LENGTH 48 in (122 cm) • HABITAT Warm
seashores • FOOD Fish • VOICE Usually silent

OFTEN SPOTTED near coastal waters,
hanging around docks or sandy beaches,
Brown Pelicans are always on the lookout
for fish. They fly low over the water in
groups when moving from place to place.
When hunting, they fly much higher, then dive
like missiles from as high as 65 feet (20 m), hitting
the water bill first and fold-
ing their wings back so they won't break them.
Underwater, the pouch balloons open to trap
fish and water. When the pelican comes to the
surface, it strains out the water and gobbles
up the fish. Brown Pelicans build their nests in
colonies, sometimes in shrubs and sometimes
on the ground.

>>> RANGE MAP

☐ BREEDING
☐ YEAR-ROUND
☐ MIGRATION

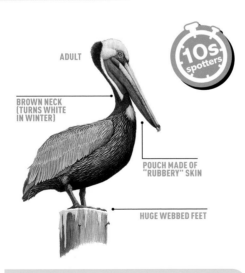

ADULT

BROWN NECK
(TURNS WHITE
IN WINTER)

POUCH MADE OF
"RUBBERY" SKIN

HUGE WEBBED FEET

10s spotters

→ **LOOK FOR THIS** When a **BROWN PELICAN'S** pouch is full
of fish, a gull will sometimes reach in and steal one before the pelican
has a chance to swallow!

TRY THIS!

A BROWN PELICAN'S
pouch can hold up to
3 gallons (11.4 L) of fish
and water. That's three
times more than its
stomach can hold. The
next time you take a
bath, bring an 8-ounce
(237-mL) plastic cup and
large cooking pot into
the tub. To fill a pelican's
pouch, you'll need to
Scoop 48 cups of
bathwater into the pot.
Now try to lift the pot.
Imagine flying with that!

GREAT BLUE HERON

Ardea herodias LENGTH 46 in (117 cm) • HABITAT Wetlands • FOOD Fish, frogs, snakes, insects, small mammals • VOICE Greeting: squawking *roh-roh-roh;* threat call: loud *FRAWNK!*

THE GREAT BLUE HERON is the largest heron in North America. Most often found in wetland areas, this long-legged bird walks through shallow water looking for fish, frogs, and insects. When it spots something, the Great Blue uses its powerful neck muscles to drive its spearlike bill into its prey. This heron's bill and neck are heavy, so as it takes off to fly, it kinks its neck back to put the weight nearer its wings. With a wingspan of 6 feet (1.8 m), it is an impressive sight. Great Blue Herons typically nest in large colonies in trees and feed their young by regurgitating fish into the nest.

>>> RANGE MAP

☐ BREEDING
☐ YEAR-ROUND
☐ WINTER

TRY THiS!

THE NEXT TIME you're playing in a shallow creek, make like a Great Blue Heron. Stand in shallow water; be as quiet and still as possible and look at the water. Do you see a water bug? A fish? Are you quick enough to catch it like a heron?

DURING BREEDING SEASON, ORNATE PLUMES ON HEAD, NECK, AND BACK OF ADULTS

10s. spotters

JUVENILE

GRAY-BLUE FEATHERS

POINTED BILL

THE WHITE-HEADED BIRD IS A VARIATION OF THE GREAT BLUE HERON FOUND IN FLORIDA AND CALLED A "WURDEMANN'S HERON"

LONG BLACK LEGS

be a BIRD NERD!

GREAT BLUE HERONS are good groomers! They have a special claw on the middle toe of each foot that has comblike teeth used for preening.

GREAT EGRET

Ardea alba LENGTH 39 in (99 cm) ▪ HABITAT Wetlands ▪ FOOD Fish, insects, reptiles, small mammals ▪ VOICE Occasionally a deep croaking *kaaark* call

IN THE LATE 19TH CENTURY, about 95 percent of all Great Egrets in North America were killed for their beautiful white plumes, which were used to decorate women's hats. Today, these tall, graceful birds have made a comeback. Great Egrets are found on every continent except Antarctica. They walk slowly through wetlands looking for fish and insects. They nest in treetops.

LONG YELLOW BILL

LONG NECK

LONG PLUMES

>>> RANGE MAP

☐ BREEDING
☐ YEAR-ROUND
☐ MIGRATION
☐ WINTER

SNOWY EGRET

Egretta thula LENGTH 24 in (61 cm) ▪ HABITAT Marshes, bays, lagoons, ponds, bayous ▪ FOOD Fish, insects, frogs, lizards ▪ VOICE Usually silent; makes a harsh croak when agitated

THE SNOWY EGRET makes its home in fresh- and saltwater bays and lagoons. It wades in shallow water looking for food, and nests in trees or shrubs near the water. Parents take turns sitting on their eggs, passing a stick to each other at the shift change. In 1886, this bird's plumes sold for $32 an ounce (28 g)—double the price of gold!

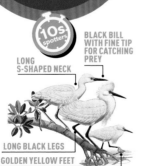

BLACK BILL WITH FINE TIP FOR CATCHING PREY

LONG S-SHAPED NECK

LONG BLACK LEGS
GOLDEN YELLOW FEET

>>> RANGE MAP

☐ BREEDING
☐ YEAR-ROUND
☐ MIGRATION
☐ WINTER

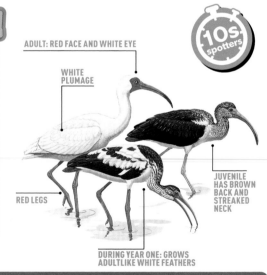

WHITE IBIS

Eudocimus albus LENGTH 25 in (64 cm) · HABITAT Swamps, beaches, coastal wetlands · FOOD Crayfish, crabs, insects, frogs · VOICE Occasional low grunts

THE WHITE IBIS makes its home in the marshes and wetlands of the Deep South. It wades through shallow water probing for crabs, crayfish, and other aquatic life and uses the sensitive tip of its bill to find its prey. This ibis is quite remarkable-looking with its scarlet face, red down-curved bill, white body, and bright red legs. White Ibises nest in large groups in trees and are strong fliers. They sometimes interbreed with the closely related Scarlet Ibis, a South American species introduced or escaped in Florida. The offspring are various shades of pink or scarlet.

>>> RANGE MAP

BREEDING
YEAR-ROUND
WINTER

be a BIRD NERD!

THE WHITE IBIS gathers in breeding colonies as big as 30,000 birds! The male shows up at the breeding grounds first, preens, and points its bill to the sky, hoping to find a mate. Once the male has a partner, it delivers building materials—like reeds, sticks, and leaves—to the female, who constructs the nest. The female lays two to five eggs and the pair take turns sitting on the nest.

10s spotters

ADULT: RED FACE AND WHITE EYE

WHITE PLUMAGE

JUVENILE HAS BROWN BACK AND STREAKED NECK

RED LEGS

DURING YEAR ONE: GROWS ADULTLIKE WHITE FEATHERS

save the birds!

Up to 44 percent of White Ibis eggs are lost to predators. Help keep the coastal waters clean. Write your senator a letter asking help to prohibit dumping sewage or medical waste in waters.

ROSEATE SPOONBILL

Platalea ajaja LENGTH 32 in (81 cm) · HABITAT Swamps, marshes
· FOOD Small fish, shrimp, aquatic insects · VOICE Mostly silent

IT'S NOT A FLAMINGO, but its colors make it look like one! The Roseate Spoonbill has red-and-pink wings, but what sets it apart from a flamingo is its distinctive flat, spoonlike bill. It uses it to sweep for food through the shallow water in marshes and wetlands. Roseate Spoonbills often roost in colonies in trees. When one flies over, a perched flock sometimes "sky gazes," with all of them extending their necks to point their bills at the sky for a few seconds. A hungry spoonbill chick gets its food by sticking its bill down a parent's throat.

>>> RANGE MAP

BREEDING

YEAR-ROUND

MIGRATION

WINTER

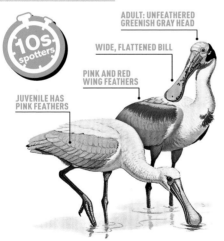

10s spotters

ADULT: UNFEATHERED GREENISH GRAY HEAD

WIDE, FLATTENED BILL

PINK AND RED WING FEATHERS

JUVENILE HAS PINK FEATHERS

→ LOOK FOR THIS
A **ROSEATE SPOONBILL** hunts for food in the early hours of morning or evening by walking slowly through shallow water with its open, spoon-shaped bill submerged. Its bill has sensitive nerve endings for feeling creatures, so it sweeps its head in wide semicircles until its bill touches a tasty morsel. Then it snaps the bill shut, and dinner is served. Members of the flock sometimes serve as "beaters," stirring up prey in the swamps and marshes for other wading spoonbills to catch. If the food has a shell, the spoonbill may beat it against a hard surface, making it easier to swallow and digest.

be a BIRD NERD!

There are five other species of SPOONBILL in the world, but they all have white plumage. Only the Roseate Spoonbill is pink.

BIRDTASTICS: Comeback Kids

A SPECIES becomes endangered when there are so few left that the species could disappear altogether. These three bird species were almost extinct, but as of 2014 there were 425 California Condors, 600 Whooping Cranes, and more than 2,000 Kirtland's Warblers counted in the United States. And the numbers are growing!

California Condor

Gymnogyps californianus

LENGTH: 47 in (119 cm)
EATS: Carcasses of land and marine animals
VOICE: Usually silent
BE A BIRD NERD: California Condors can survive up to two weeks without food!

Whooping Crane

Grus americana

LENGTH: 52 in (132 cm)
EATS: Plants, shellfish, grains
VOICE: Bugle-like call

Kirtland's Warbler

Setophaga kirtlandii

LENGTH: 5.75 in (15 cm)
EATS: Insects, fruits
VOICE: A low, strong *chip!*

CALIFORNIA CONDORS HANG OUT
ON A ROCKY CLIFF NEAR UTAH'S
ZION NATIONAL PARK. THEY
WEAR RADIO TRANSMITTERS SO
SCIENTISTS CAN KEEP TRACK
OF THEM.

TURKEY VULTURE

Cathartes aura **LENGTH** 27 in (69 cm) · **HABITAT** Wooded areas for breeding; open areas for foraging · **FOOD** Animal carcasses (carrion), including roadkill · **VOICE** Usually silent

SOMETIMES REFERRED to as a "buzzard," the Turkey Vulture is North America's most common vulture. This bird spends much of its time soaring over open areas, using its keen sense of smell to sniff out the animal carcasses it finds so tasty. Powerful stomach juices destroy disease organisms that occur in the dead meat, known as carrion. A bald head makes it easier for the vulture to clean itself up after a meal. Turkey Vultures nest on ledges or in rock crevices and thickets, away from people.

>>> RANGE MAP

BREEDING

YEAR-ROUND

MIGRATION

→ **LOOK FOR THIS**
In flight, **TURKEY VULTURES** rock from side to side and soar with wings in a V shape. When threatened, the normally quiet Turkey Vulture will hiss and also may barf in the direction of a potential predator.

BARE HEAD WITH REDDISH SKIN

JUVENILE

10S spotters

ADULT

DARK WINGS WITH SILVER FLIGHT FEATHERS

LONG TAIL

EXPERT'S CIRCLE

DON'T BE FOOLED Check out the **BLACK VULTURE** (left), southern relative of the Turkey Vulture. Darker and smaller than the Turkey Vulture, the Black Vulture has a gray head rather than a red one. This outgoing and aggressive bird doesn't have the Turkey Vulture's amazing sense of smell, so it will tag along behind one to locate a carcass. Since Black Vultures often travel in flocks, they can sometimes overpower the more solitary Turkey Vulture and take over its meal.

OSPREY

Pandion haliaetus LENGTH 24 in (61 cm) • HABITAT Rivers, smaller lakes, lagoons, bays, salt marshes • FOOD Fish • VOICE A series of chirps that are spaced out: *eeee-eeee-eeee*

THE OSPREY is a champion fisher. A type of hawk, it survives on a diet that's almost 100 percent fish. Each of the Osprey's feet has rough, spiny bottoms on the toes and four talons, helping to snag even the wiggliest fish. A pair of Ospreys shares parenting duties. The male chooses a good place for a nest that is near the water of lakes, bays, or marshes, often in a treetop or atop a power pole. He then collects sticks that the female arranges into a cozy nest. After their eggs hatch, the female tends the young while the male searches for food. A pair returns to the same nesting site year after year, adding more sticks each time until the nest becomes ginormous. Some Osprey nests can fit a person!

>>> RANGE MAP

- BREEDING
- YEAR-ROUND
- MIGRATION
- WINTER

YELLOW EYES

DARK EYE STRIPE, PROBABLY TO REDUCE GLARE OFF THE WATER

ADULT

STRONG WINGS

10s spotters

LARGE TALONS TO GRASP FISH

be a BIRD NERD!

It is the male OSPREY'S job to provide fish for the hungry young birds in the nest and few birds do it better. The Osprey may dive from as high as 100 feet (30 m) in the air, sometimes plunging so fast it folds its wings back so that its bones don't break when it hits the water. Carrying a fish in its talons, an Osprey lines it up headfirst into the wind to reduce drag and often eats the head before delivering the fish to its young. On average, an Osprey needs only 12 minutes to catch a fish. How long does it take you to catch one—or even get a nibble?

BALD EAGLE

Haliaeetus leucocephalus LENGTH 34 in (86 cm) • HABITAT Lakes, rivers, marshes, swamps, seacoasts • FOOD Fish, reptiles, small mammals, birds • VOICE A twittering *kwit kwit kee-kee-kee-kee-keer*

WE ALL KNOW the Bald Eagle as the majestic emblem of the United States, but in the early days of the nation, not everyone was a fan of this impressive bird. Benjamin Franklin believed it was a bird of "bad moral character" because it often steals food from other birds. (Franklin thought the Wild Turkey was a better candidate.) The Bald Eagle prefers fish as food, although it will also hunt small animals like reptiles, frogs, birds, and shellfish. This eagle isn't bald. The term is an old-fashioned way of referring to the white feathers of an adult eagle's head, which contrast with its brown body and wings. Usually found near water, Bald Eagles build huge stick nests high in trees, often piling more sticks on top of a previous year's nest. One nest in Ohio weighed more than 2 tons (1.8 MT)—as much as a small car! It didn't topple the tree because these eagles choose large trees and construct their nests around thick trunks and stout limb forks.

>>> RANGE MAP

BREEDING

YEAR-ROUND

MIGRATION

WINTER

Laugh Out Loud!

What kind of bird doesn't need a comb?

A bald eagle!

→ **LOOK FOR THIS**
If you spot a **BALD EAGLE** giving another bird a rough time, it isn't pulling its rank as our national bird. Instead, it may be trying to steal the other bird's hard-earned catch. Bald Eagles often target Ospreys and steal fresh-caught fish right from their talons. In general, the Bald Eagle doesn't spend much of its time in a search for food. In winter, it tends to chill in the chill, spending up to 98 percent of the time perched in a tree—perhaps wishing that Ospreys made deliveries?

10s spotters

ADULT

BILL WITH HOOKED TIP

LARGE SHARP TALONS

GOLDEN EAGLE

Aquila chrysaetos **LENGTH 35 in (89 cm)** ▪ **HABITAT Ranges from high mountains to desert** ▪ **FOOD Small mammals** ▪ **VOICE High, weak whistle during nesting season**

EVEN THOUGH it is mostly brown, the Golden Eagle gets its name from the lighter golden feathers on its head and neck. With a wingspan of 7 feet (2.1 m), this huge bird of prey soars on air currents looking for a meal—perhaps a mouse, jackrabbit, or prairie dog. Diving in for a kill, the Golden Eagle can reach a speed up to 200 miles an hour (322 km/h). Its prey hardly stands a chance. Native Americans think of the Golden Eagle as sacred. It's also the national animal of Mexico, Germany, Austria, Albania, and Kazakhstan. Golden Eagles live in a variety of habitats and build their large nests on cliffs or high in trees.

>>> RANGE MAP

☐ BREEDING
☐ YEAR-ROUND
☐ MIGRATION
☐ WINTER

HEAD AND NECK TINGED WITH GOLD

10s spotters

LARGE BILL

ADULT

FEATHERED LEGS

save the birds!

Until the 1970s, rural power lines often carried live wires that could electrocute Golden Eagles and other birds when their wings or feet made contact. Since then, utility companies have developed "raptor-safe" power lines to prevent these deaths. But now the construction of huge wind turbines to provide electrical power poses another threat. Golden Eagles often die when they fly into the enormous blades. Placing turbines off migration routes and using effective lighting can avoid this.

be a BIRD NERD!

GOLDEN EAGLES sometimes play with their food! While carrying dead prey, they may fly high into the sky, drop it, and then race down to retrieve it.

COOPER'S HAWK

Accipiter cooperii LENGTH **17 in (43 cm)** • HABITAT **Woodlands, suburbs, towns** • FOOD **Small birds, often ones eating at feeders** • VOICE **Nasal series of *kek* notes**

A SKILLED FLIER, the Cooper's Hawk uses its long, rounded tail like a rudder to make speedy turns and navigate through woodlands. More and more, this hawk is found in urban areas, nesting in large shade trees. It picks off small birds that visit backyard feeders and may even chase its prey on foot through dense vegetation.

>>> RANGE MAP

BREEDING

YEAR-ROUND

WINTER

ADULT

DARK CAP

REDDISH BARS ON UNDERPARTS

LONG TAIL WITH BLACK BARS AND ROUNDED TIP

10s spotters

....

RED-SHOULDERED HAWK

Buteo lineatus LENGTH **17 in (43 cm)** • HABITAT **Woodlands, especially near water; swamps** • FOOD **Small mammals, frogs, snakes** • VOICE **Loud *kee-yer*, often in flight**

THE RED-SHOULDERED HAWK takes a wait-and-see approach to hunting: It perches quietly in a tree and then drops down on the frog, snake, or small mammal it wants for a meal. This aggressive bird sometimes takes on other hawks and Great Horned Owls, locking talons with them in midair! Migrating Red-shouldered Hawks often join other hawks in large groups.

ADULT

BLACK-AND-WHITE PATTERN ON WINGS AND TAIL

REDDISH BARS ON CHEST, SHOULDERS, AND UNDERWINGS

10s spotters

>>> RANGE MAP

BREEDING

YEAR-ROUND

MIGRATION

WINTER

RED-TAILED HAWK

Buteo jamaicensis LENGTH 22 in (56 cm) • HABITAT Mountains, woodlands, prairies, deserts • FOOD Small mammals, reptiles, birds • VOICE A harsh, descending *keee-eerrrrr*

ON YOUR NEXT ROAD TRIP, keep a steady watch from the car window and you may spot a Red-tailed Hawk. The most common hawk in North America, this bird flies over open fields looking for prey like mice, voles, snakes, and lizards. The Red-tailed Hawk lives nearly everywhere, from woodlands to prairies to deserts to large cities. For more than two decades, the adventures of a Red-tail known as Pale Male have entertained visitors to New York's Central Park. This species usually finds a high place to nest, such as a large tree, cliff, or ledge of a high-rise building. The plumage of Red-tails differs a lot, depending on location. An Alaska population is almost completely black, while a population that nests on the Great Plains is very pale.

>>> RANGE MAP

BREEDING

YEAR-ROUND

WINTER

10s spotters

LARGE, DARK EYES

ADULT

BROAD, ROUNDED WINGS

ADULT'S "RED" TAIL IS MORE OF A RUSTY BROWN COLOR

→ LOOK FOR THIS

RED-TAILS adapt to city life and raise their families there. Watch for them in a city park or perched on the ledge of a tall building. A Red-tailed Hawk's harsh call is very distinctive. It's so eerie and penetrating that it often is used as the wilderness sound in movies and television programs set in the Old West. Think back to the shows you've seen and you're sure to remember this sound. In cities, these spooky tones can also be heard above the traffic.

be a BIRD NERD!

RED-TAILED HAWKS display dramatic courtship behavior. A courting pair may circle high in the sky, clasp talons, and then spiral together toward the ground. They separate before bottoming out.

AMERICAN KESTREL

Falco sparverius LENGTH **10.5 in (27 cm)** • HABITAT **Open country, farmlands, deserts** • FOOD **Mice, insects, other small prey** • VOICE **A shrill, rapid** *killy killy killy*

IT MAY LOOK LIKE A HAWK, but the American Kestrel is a falcon—a member of a group more closely related to parrots and songbirds. The most common falcon in North America, the American Kestrel is petite, with a rusty brown body and "sideburns"—a dark, double stripe on each side of the face. Check out the female at left. Kestrels live and hunt in open areas with low vegetation and short trees and also in meadows, deserts, and suburban areas. For nests they often prefer tree cavities that are pre-dug by woodpeckers, and will also move into nest boxes. While on the hunt, kestrels may hover in place, scoping out the ground below for prey. They even see ultraviolet light, which allows them to locate urine-marked trails made by rodents.

>>> RANGE MAP

☐ BREEDING
☐ YEAR-ROUND
☐ MIGRATION
☐ WINTER

be a BIRD NERD!

American Kestrels are fast, nimble fliers and are known as fierce predators, but they also face danger. The tables can turn and they can become the prey for larger birds like Red-tailed Hawks, Barn Owls, and American Crows. While they're searching for insects and other prey in open territory, kestrels usually perch on wires or poles—in plain view. Bigger hunters can easily swoop down after catching a glimpse of a kestrel flapping its wings and adjusting its tail to stay in place on its perch. On the ground, Rat Snakes and Corn Snakes will also go after kestrels.

DOUBLE BLACK STRIPES ON A WHITE FACE

10S. spotters

RUSTY BROWN BACK AND TAIL

MALE

LONG, SQUARE-TIPPED TAIL

→ **LOOK FOR THIS** Football fans? **AMERICAN KESTRELS** occasionally "attend" nighttime sporting events. Perched on lights and foul poles, they hunt for moths and other insects attracted to bright stadium lights.

PEREGRINE FALCON

Falco peregrinus **LENGTH 18 in (46 cm)** · **HABITAT Tundra, coastal areas, open wetlands, cities** · **FOOD Mostly birds** · **VOICE Makes harsh** *cack* **sounds when agitated**

WITH ITS DARK, "helmeted" head, the Peregrine Falcon breaks all bird speed records. In a vertical dive, known as a stoop, it can clock 200 miles an hour (322 km/h). It can give chase to prey at 70 miles an hour (113 km/h) and easily maintains a traveling speed of 30 miles an hour (48 km/h).

It hunts birds of many sizes, from humming-birds to Sandhill Cranes. The name "peregrine" means "wanderer" or "pilgrim"—it fits this bird that lives on every continent except Antarctica. Peregrines were long known to nest on cliffs, but now they also build their nests on bridges and ledges of tall buildings.

>>> RANGE MAP

BREEDING
YEAR-ROUND
MIGRATION
WINTER

10s spotters

DARK WEDGE OF FEATHERS BELOW THE EYE

ADULT

LARGE FEET WITH SHARP TALONS

ADULT HAS BLUE-GRAY BACK AND WINGS, AND A BLACKISH HOOD

be a BIRD NERD!

The **PEREGRINE FALCON** attacks by diving down from high above. It uses powerful feet to stun or kill prey, but before the helpless target can hit the ground, the falcon swoops down and grabs it. Then the Peregrine flies its kill off to a secure dining spot and has a meal. Humans have hunted with falcons for more than 2,000 years. Sometimes the Peregrines themselves are the prey, hunted by larger birds such as eagles, Great Horned Owls, and Gyrfalcons.

VIRGINIA RAIL

Rallus limicola LENGTH 9.5 in (24 cm) • HABITAT Freshwater and coastal marshes • FOOD Insects, fish, frogs, small snakes • VOICE A series of *kid kid kidick kidick* notes and a *tic tic turrr*

ALTHOUGH THE Virginia Rail is pretty common in North America, it's not often seen because it hides in dense reeds along freshwater and salt marshes. The rails push through so many tight spaces that their forehead feathers have adapted for the wear and tear.

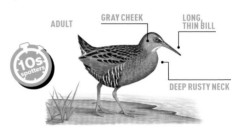

ADULT | GRAY CHEEK | LONG, THIN BILL

DEEP RUSTY NECK

>>> RANGE MAP

BREEDING
YEAR-ROUND
MIGRATION
WINTER

SORA

Porzana carolina LENGTH 8.75 in (22 cm) • HABITAT Shallow wetlands, grain fields • FOOD Seeds, aquatic insects • VOICE A descending whinny and a high-pitched *keek*

IF YOU CAN get close enough to recognize a Sora by its yellow bill, you're lucky. Although they're the most common rail in North America, Soras stay hidden in cattails and other dense vegetation. Known as "meadow chickens," Soras can compress their bodies to slip quietly through tight spaces. They're hunted by hawks and coyotes in fall when they've fattened up on wild rice.

THICK YELLOW BILL

BREEDING ADULT

BREEDING BIRDS HAVE A BLACKISH FACE AND NECK

>>> RANGE MAP

BREEDING
YEAR-ROUND
MIGRATION
WINTER

AMERICAN COOT

Fulica americana LENGTH **15.5 in (39 cm)** · HABITAT **Fresh and salt open waters** · FOOD **Aquatic plants, insects, aquatic animals** · VOICE **Grunting and clucking calls**

IT LOOKS LIKE A DUCK and swims like a duck, but the American Coot is a closer relative of the Sandhill Crane. Instead of webbed feet, the coot has long toes with lobes of skin that help it swim. American Coots live in a variety of open-water habitats—from lakes to wetlands to sewage ponds. They mostly eat aquatic plants, but they also will eat insects, snails, and crustaceans. They use vegetation to build nests over water, but sometimes will lay their eggs in the nests of other birds. In winter, they may gather in flocks numbering in the thousands.

>>> **RANGE MAP**

BREEDING

YEAR-ROUND

MIGRATION

WINTER

ADULT

MOSTLY WHITE BILL

CHARCOAL GRAY WITH BLACKER HEAD

LOBED TOES

EXPERT'S CIRCLE

DON'T BE FOOLED The **COMMON GALLINULE** (left) can be spotted in marshes and ponds from Canada to Chile and is often mistaken for the American Coot. It's a similar size, but is black with a red forehead shield and yellow bill tip. Long toes help it walk in mud and floating vegetation. It eats mostly seeds and some snails, and builds a nest of grasses near the water's edge. Common Gallinules have plenty to say: They cluck, whinny, cackle, and squawk.

SANDHILL CRANE

Grus canadensis **LENGTH** 46 in (117 cm) · **HABITAT** Marshes, tundra, grain fields, wetlands · **FOOD** Grain, seeds, insects · **VOICE** Loud, trumpeting *gar-oo-oo*

MANY PEOPLE MISTAKE the Great Blue Heron for the Sandhill Crane. But the slate gray Sandhill has a distinct look and sound. Tail feathers droop over its rump, like a bustle (underwear worn in the 1800s to make ladies' dresses look full in the back), and its head has bare, bumpy skin on the crown that turns bright red in breeding season. The Great Blue Heron lacks the bustle and red skin, but has long neck, back, and head plumes when breeding. Also, cranes trumpet and herons squawk. The cranes build nests from marsh vegetation close to the water. Chicks leave the nest about eight hours after hatching and go wading! They stay with mom and dad for about a year.

>>> RANGE MAP

BREEDING

YEAR-ROUND

MIGRATION

WINTER

TRY THiS!

CAN YOU WALK

like a courting Sandhill Crane? It's easy … sort of. Stretch out your arms as if they were wings, then bob your head and bow before leaping into the air like a graceful ballerina. (You'll get the hang of it.) Their spectacular leaps are accompanied by calls. They end up with mates who like their moves.

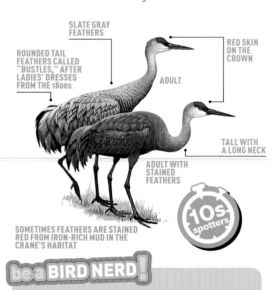

SLATE GRAY FEATHERS

RED SKIN ON THE CROWN

ROUNDED TAIL FEATHERS CALLED "BUSTLES," AFTER LADIES' DRESSES FROM THE 1800s

ADULT

TALL WITH A LONG NECK

ADULT WITH STAINED FEATHERS

SOMETIMES FEATHERS ARE STAINED RED FROM IRON-RICH MUD IN THE CRANE'S HABITAT

10s spotters

be a BIRD NERD!

In early spring, about half a million CRANES gather along the Platte River in Nebraska to fatten up before migrating north.

KILLDEER

Charadrius vociferus LENGTH **10.5 in (27 cm)** ▪ HABITAT **Open fields, and sometimes along shores** ▪ FOOD **Earthworms, grasshoppers, beetles** ▪ VOICE **Loud *kill-dee***

KILLDEER were named for the unique sound they make—a piercing *kill-dee!* This widespread member of the plover family can be spotted in open fields and even on lawns and in parking lots. It eats mostly spineless creatures such as earthworms, snails, grasshoppers, beetles, and crayfish. Killdeer build simple nests right on the ground and add a few rocks, sticks, or other debris. If a predator comes near the nest, a Killdeer sometimes fakes a broken wing to lure it away from its eggs or babies.

>>> RANGE MAP

- BREEDING
- YEAR-ROUND
- MIGRATION
- WINTER

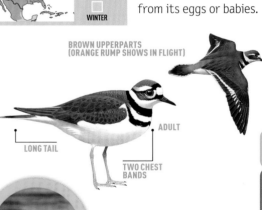

BROWN UPPERPARTS (ORANGE RUMP SHOWS IN FLIGHT)

ADULT

LONG TAIL

TWO CHEST BANDS

10 s spotters

EXPERT'S CIRCLE

DON'T BE FOOLED A relative of the Killdeer, the **SEMIPALMATED PLOVER** (left) gets its name from its partially webbed (semipalmated) feet. It hangs around beaches and lakeshores, looking for small insects to eat. This plover has a brown back and a white chest with a single band. Its short, orange bill has a black tip. The Semipalmated Plover builds its nest on the ground, using bits of leaves and other debris. Its call is a whistled *chu-weet*.

save
the birds!

Killdeer are attracted to playing fields, parking lots, and gravel rooftops to make their nests. The gravel mimics the ground where they usually build nests, and the roof puts them out of reach of some predators. But it's a dangerous trade-off. Rooftops are not a good place for chicks, which will have a long drop to the ground if they fall before they've learned to fly.

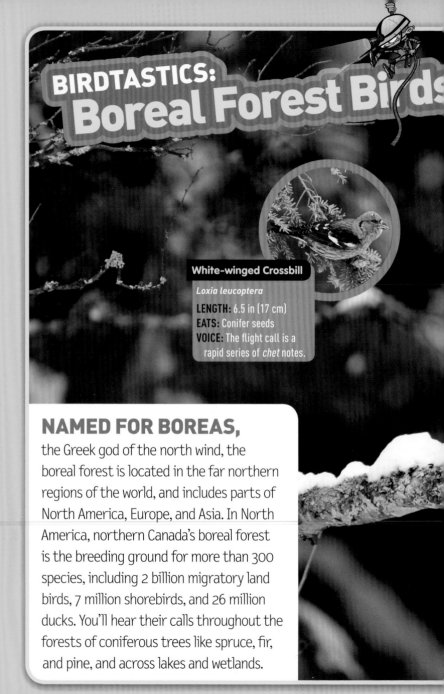

BIRDTASTICS:
Boreal Forest Birds

White-winged Crossbill

Loxia leucoptera
LENGTH: 6.5 in (17 cm)
EATS: Conifer seeds
VOICE: The flight call is a
rapid series of *chet* notes.

NAMED FOR BOREAS,

the Greek god of the north wind, the boreal forest is located in the far northern regions of the world, and includes parts of North America, Europe, and Asia. In North America, northern Canada's boreal forest is the breeding ground for more than 300 species, including 2 billion migratory land birds, 7 million shorebirds, and 26 million ducks. You'll hear their calls throughout the forests of coniferous trees like spruce, fir, and pine, and across lakes and wetlands.

A GREAT GRAY OWL PERCHES ON A BRANCH IN A BOREAL FOREST IN THE SCANDINAVIAN COUNTRY OF FINLAND.

Great Gray Owl

Strix nebulosa

LENGTH: 27 in (69 cm)
EATS: Small mammals, like mice and voles
VOICE: Call is a series of deep *whoo* notes.
BE A BIRD NERD: The Great Gray Owl has the largest wingspan of any North American owl—up to 5 feet (1.5 m)!

Spruce Grouse

Falcipennis canadensis

LENGTH: 16 in (41 cm)
EATS: Pine and spruce needles
VOICE: Soft, clucking notes

SPOTTED SANDPIPER

Actitis macularius **LENGTH 7.5 in (19 cm)** ◦ **HABITAT Freshwater habitats and along seacoasts** ◦ **FOOD Insects, including mayflies, grasshoppers, beetles** ◦ **VOICE A shrill *peet-weet***

SPOTTED SANDPIPERS are small, distinct-looking birds that are often seen walking along the shorelines of lakes and rivers, ponds, and seacoasts. They are brown on the back with noticeable spots on their white chest during breeding season. When surprised by predators, Spotted Sandpipers pretend to be injured and make a squeaking sound as they move away from their nesting area to protect their eggs from attack. They use their beak to hunt for insects, like mayflies and grasshoppers. The birds nest near the water, usually under the shade of a leafy plant. The Spotted Sandpiper's call is either a shrill *peet-weet* or a series of *weet* notes.

>>> RANGE MAP

- BREEDING
- YEAR-ROUND
- MIGRATION
- WINTER

be a BIRD NERD!

Uncommonly for a North American sandpiper, the breeding range of the SPOTTED SANDPIPER covers much of the continent. Parenting in this species is mostly the male's work. Dad provides much of the day care and the chicks stay with him for at least four weeks. A female may abandon the family to start a new nest and create a new family with another mate.

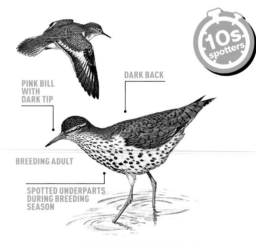

PINK BILL WITH DARK TIP

DARK BACK

10s spotters

BREEDING ADULT

SPOTTED UNDERPARTS DURING BREEDING SEASON

MALES AND FEMALES LOOK SIMILAR

→ **LOOK FOR THIS** The **SPOTTED SANDPIPER** is known as a "teeter-tail." When it walks it teeter-totters! The bird is awkward in flight, too: It flies with stiff, stuttering wingbeats.

LONG-BILLED CURLEW

Numenius americanus LENGTH 23 in (58 cm) · HABITAT Prairies, farmlands; in winter, mudflats, wetlands · FOOD Shrimp, crabs, insects, earthworms · VOICE Musical *cur-lee*

THE LARGEST SHOREBIRD in North America, the Long-billed Curlew is noticed for its superlong bill. The bill equals a third of its body length. It comes in very handy for poking around as the curlew wades in shallow water to find shrimp and crabs or digs in a pasture for worms. The Long-billed Curlew prefers to nest in shortgrass prairies and meadows and it winters near tidal mudflats, lakeshores, and croplands.

>>> RANGE MAP

BREEDING
MIGRATION
WINTER

LONG, DOWN-CURVED BILL

ADULT

BODY IS CINNAMON BROWN

FEATHERS HAVE DARK STRIPES OR BARS

10s spotters

save the birds!

The number of Long-billed Curlews is declining on the Great Plains, due mainly to land development. Large areas of grassland are being replaced by farmland and new houses. Also, pesticide spray kills off a lot of the curlews' insect food, including tasty grasshoppers.

be a BIRD NERD!

A male LONG-BILLED CURLEW offers his mate a choice of shallow nesting spots that he has prepared. When she chooses one, they finish the nest by digging the hole a bit deeper and adding a lining of grasses, twigs, pebbles—and even dried cow dung or other animal droppings. Then it's up to her to lay a group of eggs—called a clutch—in the customized nest.

GREATER YELLOWLEGS

Tringa melanoleuca LENGTH 14 in (36 cm) • HABITAT Freshwater ponds, tidal marshes • FOOD Insects, minnows • VOICE Series of *tew* notes

THE GREATER YELLOWLEGS has—you guessed it—yellow legs. A common shorebird, the Greater Yellowlegs is found near ponds, tidal marshes, and forest clearings. It eats insects and small aquatic life, like fish and frogs, and searches for food by sweeping its bill from side to side until it feels something. It also feeds on seeds and berries. When disturbed, it gets dramatic and makes piercing alarm calls.

>>> RANGE MAP

BREEDING

MIGRATION

WINTER

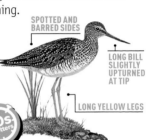

SPOTTED AND BARRED SIDES

LONG BILL SLIGHTLY UPTURNED AT TIP

LONG YELLOW LEGS

LESSER YELLOWLEGS

Tringa flavipes LENGTH 10.5 in (27 cm) • HABITAT Tundra, woodlands; in winter, near fresh and salt water • FOOD Insects, minnows, seeds • VOICE One or more *tew* notes

THE LESSER YELLOWLEGS—similar to the Greater Yellowlegs, but smaller—can be seen running through shallow water to chase down its preferred food, such as insects and small fish. This species breeds in the northern areas of North America and spends the winter in coastal and freshwater habitats.

BILL SLIGHTLY LONGER THAN HEAD

SPOTTED AND BARRED SIDES

YELLOW LEGS

>>> RANGE MAP

BREEDING

MIGRATION

WINTER

RUDDY TURNSTONE

Arenaria interpres LENGTH 9.5 in (24 cm) · HABITAT Coastal tundra, mudflats, sandy and rocky shores · FOOD Aquatic invertebrates, insects · VOICE A short, chuckling rattle

THE RUDDY TURNSTONE gets its name from the reddish (ruddy) color on its back and from its habit of flipping over stones, shells, and seaweed with its bill to search for food. On the buggy coastal tundra during the summer breeding season, this species eats mostly flies. Yum! Like many other shorebirds, turnstones build nests on the ground.

>>> RANGE MAP

BREEDING

MIGRATION

WINTER

BLACK-AND-WHITE FACE WITH A BAND ON ITS NECK

SHORT ORANGE LEGS

REDDISH BACK AND WINGS DURING BREEDING SEASON

SANDERLING

Calidris alba LENGTH 8 in (20 cm) · HABITAT Breeds in the tundra of the Arctic and migrates to seacoast beaches · FOOD Small crabs, mollusks, crab eggs · VOICE Males have a froglike trill; females make a series of buzzing noises

SANDERLINGS are beach lovers. Most of the year they can be found up and down the Atlantic and Pacific coasts looking for food they find at the water's edge. They probe the wet sand with their stout beaks, looking for small animals, like sand crabs. They nest in the Arctic tundra.

STOUT BILL

BLACK LEGS

LIGHT GRAY BACK AND WINGS AND WHITE CHEST DURING WINTER

>>> RANGE MAP

BREEDING

MIGRATION

WINTER

AMERICAN WOODCOCK

Scolopax minor LENGTH **11 in (28 cm)** • HABITAT **Shrubby forests and fields** • FOOD **Earthworms and other invertebrates like snails, spiders, and ants** • VOICE **A nasal *peent***

THE AMERICAN WOODCOCK wears its own camouflage. Its brown, mottled feathers blend perfectly with dead leaves on the forest floor. The woodcock leads a secretive life, searching for food at night. It nests on the ground in the open. You're most likely to see one at dawn and dusk. But you have to be very quiet. The woodcock startles easily and will dart up if it is disturbed.

The woodcock uses its long bill to probe the soil of forests and fields. It searches for the earthworms, millipedes, snails, and other invertebrates—along with bits of plants—that make up its diet.

>>> RANGE MAP

- BREEDING
- YEAR-ROUND
- MIGRATION
- WINTER

→ LOOK FOR THIS

AMERICAN WOODCOCKS have eyes in the back of their heads. Well, practically. The woodcock's eyes are near the rear of its skull so it can find predators flying above. That's important because the bird spends a lot of its time with its head down, probing for food. At mating time, the male woodcock gives a buzzy *peent* call from the ground. Then he flies up in a spiral pattern, slowly zigzags down while chirping, and lands beside a female.

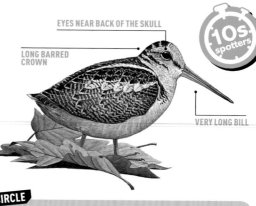

EYES NEAR BACK OF THE SKULL

LONG BARRED CROWN

VERY LONG BILL

10s spotters

EXPERT'S CIRCLE

DON'T BE FOOLED Stocky with a boldly striped head, the **WILSON'S SNIPE** (left) has extra-strong breast muscles that allow it to fly at a speed of 60 miles an hour (97 km/h). This sandpiper lives in wet marshy habitats like bogs and swamps and along rivers and lakes. It has a much larger range in North America than the American Woodcock.

ATLANTIC PUFFIN

Fratercula arctica LENGTH 12.5 in (32 cm) • HABITAT Rocky islands in the North Atlantic • FOOD Fish • VOICE Growling notes when at its breeding colony

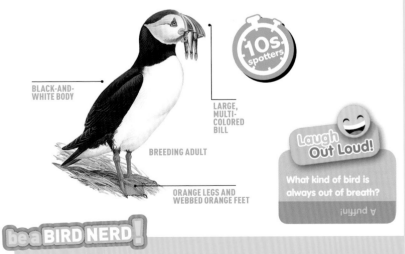

CALLED THE "CLOWN OF THE SEA" for its comical face with a multicolored bill, the Atlantic Puffin looks a little like a penguin. But despite a stocky build and black-and-white plumage, the Atlantic Puffin is a member of a family of seabirds called auks. Puffins fly and they also swim underwater, chasing after small fish, their main source of food. Atlantic Puffins breed on rocky islands off the coast of Maine and farther north. They dig nests in the ground with the help of their large bills, using their webbed feet like shovels. A single egg is laid in the nest. Atlantic Puffins were hunted heavily for their meat in the 1800s and many colonies were wiped out by the early 1900s. Today, conservation efforts are bringing these amazing birds back home.

>>> RANGE MAP

- BREEDING
- YEAR-ROUND
- MIGRATION
- WINTER

BLACK-AND-WHITE BODY

LARGE, MULTI-COLORED BILL

BREEDING ADULT

ORANGE LEGS AND WEBBED ORANGE FEET

10s spotters

Laugh Out Loud!

What kind of bird is always out of breath?

A puffin!

bea BIRD NERD!

The ATLANTIC PUFFIN can hold more than a dozen small, slippery fish in its bill at one time.

TUFTED PUFFIN

Fratercula cirrhata LENGTH 16 in (41 cm) · HABITAT Open water, islands, cliffs along the north Pacific coast · FOOD Fish · VOICE Low grumbling notes when in its breeding colony

THE TUFTED PUFFIN is named for its most notable feature: long pale golden yellow tufts that sweep back from the sides of the adult's head during mating season. These fish-eaters breed along the Pacific coast, from northern California northward, and spend winters at sea.

>>> RANGE MAP

BREEDING

MIGRATION

WINTER

LONG PALE YELLOW HEAD TUFTS

BRIGHT ORANGE BILL

BREEDING ADULT

DARK UNDERPARTS

MARBLED MURRELET

Brachyramphus marmoratus length 10 in (25 cm) · HABITAT Breeds in forests near the coast; northern birds nest on the ground in rock crevices · FOOD Fish · VOICE Loud, high *kree* notes

THE MARBLED MURRELET is a seabird of the northern Pacific. Unlike other seabirds, it often nests inland, building its home high in the branches of trees in old-growth coastal forests. It winters along the coast. The Marbled Murrelet feeds on fish, diving underwater and using its wings to swim after them. This species is vocal year-round, making loud *kree* sounds.

BLACK CAP AND WHITE COLLAR

WHITE UNDERPARTS

MALE IN WINTER

>>> RANGE MAP

BREEDING

YEAR-ROUND

WINTER

LAUGHING GULL

Leucophaeus atricilla **LENGTH 16.5 in (42 cm)** · **HABITAT Mostly along Gulf and Atlantic coasts** · **FOOD Almost anything, from fish to fast food** · **VOICE A series of *hah* notes**

IF YOU'VE EVER SEEN some gulls gathered in your supermarket parking lot, you know that not all "seagulls" live near the sea. But the Laughing Gull is seldom far from salt water. Named for its flight call—a crowing series of *hah* notes—the Laughing Gull is a common sight on Atlantic and Gulf coast beaches. It spends a lot of time searching for food and is not at all picky about what it eats. It follows fishing boats to snag bait, visits picnic blankets looking for a handout, scrounges food from landfills, and even steals fish from pelicans. At times it will hover in the air to feed on flying insects. Laughing Gulls nest on saltwater marshes, islands, and sandy beaches, forming colonies of up to 25,000 pairs.

>>> **RANGE MAP**

BREEDING
YEAR-ROUND
MIGRATION
WINTER

RED BILL

BLACK HOOD

IN WINTER, HEAD IS MOSTLY WHITE AND BILL IS BLACKISH

BREEDING ADULT

LONG WINGS

10s spotters

→ **LOOK FOR THIS** Early in the nesting season, **LAUGHING GULLS** sometimes hold swim parties. They gather in large groups and spend a bit of time dipping and dunking themselves while making a lot of noise. Water can be dangerous to gull chicks in their nests, though. A nest needs to be far enough away from the shoreline so that when the tide comes in their home stays safe from flooding.

Laugh Out Loud!

Why do some seagulls fly over the sea?

Because if they flew over the bay, they'd be called bagels!

RING-BILLED GULL

Larus delawarensis LENGTH **17.5 in (45 cm)** • HABITAT **Urban and agricultural areas, coastal waters** • FOOD **Fish, worms, insects, rodents, human garbage** • VOICE **A mewing *kee-ew* and a sharp *kyow***

RING-BILLED GULLS are the most common "seagulls" across North America, but only some of them spend any time at sea. They usually nest on the ground near freshwater in a colony of pairs that can number up to the tens of thousands. They've adapted well to the human environment. You can check out the familiar black band circling their yellow bill—and yellow feet to match—at their favorite hangouts: at landfills, outside fast-food restaurants (guard those fries!), and in freshly mowed farm fields. They also show up at more traditional places, including beaches, estuaries, and mudflats, as well as at docks. (Why go fishing when a boat will deliver it to you?) Ring-billed Gulls eat anything and everything—from insects to fish to berries to hamburger buns. Although this species was nearly wiped out a century ago, it is now so abundant that the gulls are regarded as serious pests in some areas.

>>> RANGE MAP

BREEDING
YEAR-ROUND
MIGRATION
WINTER

TRY THIS!

THE NEXT TIME you're planning a picnic at the beach, try this trick to keep unwanted Ring-billed Gulls and other pesky birds away from your blanket. Purchase a plastic or wooden owl from a garden center and pack it with your gear. Display the owl while you eat. Gulls often avoid these bird-of-prey decoys and will move along!

BLACK BAND ON YELLOW BILL

10S spotters

ADULTS HAVE GRAY BACK AND WINGS, AND WHITE CHEST

WHITE BODY

BREEDING ADULT

YELLOW LEGS

HERRING GULL

Larus argentatus LENGTH **25 in (64 cm)** ○ HABITAT **Widespread along coasts and inland** ○ FOOD **Marine invertebrates, fish, other birds, carrion** ○ VOICE **Loud** *kyow*

HERRING GULLS are hardy birds. That means they're tough. They are adapted to many environments and have many survival skills. They can drink ocean water when no freshwater is available—their nasal glands excrete the excess salt. They can handle almost any kind of weather, and will eat just about anything—from fish to worms to garbage. Once their chicks hatch, parents feed them for about three months.

YELLOW BILL WITH A RED SPOT

ADULTS IN WINTER HAVE A STREAKED HEAD AND NECK

PINK LEGS

YOUNG ARE A SPOTTY BROWN COLOR WITH A DARK-TIPPED BILL

>>> RANGE MAP

BREEDING

YEAR-ROUND

MIGRATION

WINTER

WESTERN GULL

Larus occidentalis LENGTH **25 in (64 cm)** ○ HABITAT **Along the Pacific coast; breeds on rocky islands** ○ FOOD **Fish, marine invertebrates, eggs and chicks of other seabirds** ○ VOICE **A low whistly** *kyow*

WESTERN GULLS stick close to the coastline of the Pacific Ocean, hunting for fish and marine invertebrates. They'll grab an opportunity to steal food from other birds, seals—and your picnic table. They also raid the nests of other birds for eggs and chicks. These large gulls breed on rocky islands, making nests on cliffs out of vegetation and feathers.

YELLOW BILL WITH A RED SPOT

PINK LEGS

BREEDING ADULT

>>> RANGE MAP

YEAR-ROUND

WINTER

CASPIAN TERN

Hydroprogne caspia LENGTH 21 in (53 cm) · HABITAT Large lakes and marshes; winters on southern coasts · FOOD Mostly fish · VOICE Loud, raspy *kowk* and *ca-arr*

AS LARGE AS A GULL, the Caspian Tern is the largest tern in the world. It cruises above the water searching for fish, its main food source. When it spots a fish, the tern dives headfirst and snatches it in its bill. Caspian Terns breed in colonies along coastal tidal marshes and island beaches. They build nests on the ground and aggressively defend their chicks from predators—and people!

>>> RANGE MAP

BREEDING

YEAR-ROUND

MIGRATION

WINTER

10s spotters

BLACK CROWN CHANGES TO STREAKED BROWN IN WINTER

LARGE CORAL RED BILL

WINTER ADULT

COMMON TERN

Sterna hirundo LENGTH 14.5 in (37 cm) · HABITAT Islands, marshes, some ocean beaches and lakes · FOOD Small fish and invertebrates · VOICE Sharp *kip* and a low, drawn-out *kee-ar-r-r-r*

THE COMMON TERN, as its name suggest, is the most common tern found in North America. It can be found along marshes, lakes, ocean beaches, and on islands. This delicate tern drinks in flight, gliding low over the water and dipping in its bill from time to time. Like many seabirds, it can drink salt water. To fish for food, it hovers over the water, and then plunges in.

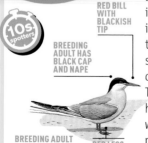

RED BILL WITH BLACKISH TIP

BREEDING ADULT HAS BLACK CAP AND NAPE

10s spotters

BREEDING ADULT

RED LEGS

>>> RANGE MAP

BREEDING

MIGRATION

WINTER

BLACK SKIMMER

Rynchops niger LENGTH 18 in (46 cm) • HABITAT Sandy beaches, salt marshes, lagoons • FOOD Mostly fish, occasionally small crabs and shrimp • VOICE *Nasal ip or yep*

NO, THIS BIRD doesn't have a broken bill—it's made that way! The Black Skimmer has a knifelike red-and-black bill that is much longer on the bottom half than on the top. The unusual look has a purpose. The Black Skimmer flies close to the water's surface and lets its lower bill drop just below it. When the bill touches a fish, the upper bill snaps shut. Then the skimmer gobbles up the fish. Black Skimmers will travel as many as 5 miles (8 km) in search of fish. These sociable birds like to hang out together. They nest in colonies on sandy beaches and form large flocks the rest of the year. They tend to be loners when they search for food, though. Because of the unusual bill, they've earned such nicknames as "Cut-Water," "Knifebill," and "Scissorbill."

>>> RANGE MAP

BREEDING

YEAR-ROUND

MIGRATION

WINTER

LONG WINGS WITH BLACK-AND-WHITE PATTERN

RED BILL WITH BLACK TIP

EXTRA-LONG LOWER BILL

be a BIRD NERD!

BLACK SKIMMERS mostly forage at dawn and dusk, and even at night. They can feed under the moonlight because they find their food by touch. Fish tend to be closer to the surface when it's dark. When fishing by day, the skimmer's slit-like pupils can be mostly closed to protect its eyes from sunlight and glare. Who needs sunglasses when you're a Black Skimmer?

→ **LOOK FOR THIS** Because it often hunts during the evening hours, the **BLACK SKIMMER** sits around much of the day in tightly packed flocks. Tough life!

BIRDTASTICS:
Champion Birds

TALK ABOUT SUPERSTARS! These three birds take the prize in the categories of distance, weight, and chattiness. No longer than two stacked pencils, the Bar-tailed Godwits leave Alaska and migrate across most of the Pacific Ocean all the way to New Zealand—that's 7,512 miles (12,089 km)! The Mute Swan pictured here may not have much to say, but it's a true heavyweight. One of the largest flying birds in North America, it weighs up to 31.5 pounds (14.3 kg). Male Red-eyed Vireos sing 30 different songs, and sing them up to 22,000 times in a single day!

Bar-tailed Godwit

Limosa lapponica

LENGTH: 16 in (41 cm)
EATS: Insects, worms, seeds, berries
VOICE: Call is *Pid-wid*

Red-eyed Vireo

Vireo olivaceus

LENGTH: 6 in (15 cm)
EATS: Insects, seeds, fruits
VOICE: Whining *quee* call

Mute Swan

Cygnus olor

LENGTH: 60 in (152 cm)
EATS: Aquatic plants and animals
VOICE: Snorting *heorrr* call
LIFE SPAN: 34 years (in the wild)
BE A BIRD NERD: When swimming,
Mute Swans point their bills down,
and their necks form an S shape.

MUTE SWANS LIKE THIS ONE WERE
BROUGHT FROM EUROPE TO GRACE THE
PONDS AND LAKES OF ESTATES.

ROCK PIGEON

Columba livia **LENGTH** 12.5 in (32 cm) • **HABITAT** City streets, parks, rural farm buildings • **FOOD** Seeds, crumbs that are found or fed to them • **VOICE** Call is throaty *cooing*

ROCK PIGEONS were first brought to America by European settlers 400 years ago. Now, they are a common sight in cities all over the world, pecking for crumbs and seeds on sidewalks and in parks. They are generally bluish gray with two dark wing bars, although many variations exist—from pure white to rusty brown. Most Rock Pigeons live near people, often building their nests on building ledges. During courtship, they make a *coo-cuk-cuk-cuk-cooo* sound. Many people breed, train, and race pigeons.

>>> RANGE MAP

YEAR-ROUND

MOST HAVE TWO DARK BARS, LIKE STRIPES, ACROSS THEIR WINGS AND A WHITE RUMP

10s spotters

RED EYES

PINK LEGS AND FEET

GLOSSY NECK

True or False

Q: A pigeon was given a medal for being a war hero.

A: TRUE! G.I. Joe, a World War II carrier pigeon, was given a special medal after delivering a message that prevented an Allied-occupied Italian village from being bombed.

Q: Pigeons never nest in the same place twice.

A: FALSE! Pigeons reuse their nests over and over, and each time they grow larger and sturdier.

be a BIRD NERD!

Pigeons are able to find their way home—even when blindfolded—by sensing the Earth's magnetic field.

MOURNING DOVE

Zenaida macroura **LENGTH 12 in (31 cm)** • **HABITAT Rural and residential areas, deserts, fields** • **FOOD Mostly seeds** • **VOICE Slow, mournful *oowoo-woo-woo-woo* call**

MOURNING DOVES are one of the most abundant land birds in the United States and are known for their distinctive, mournful *coo*. Found in open spaces in both rural and residential areas, Mourning Doves have a diet that is made up almost entirely of seeds. They eat up to 20 percent of their body weight in a day! Their flimsy nests, made of twigs and sticks, can be found on tree branches or on the ground. When they fly, their wings make a whistling sound. Mourning Doves are plump with long tails and short legs. They are brown or tan-colored with black spots on their wings and tail feathers. They are often seen perched on telephone wires.

>>> RANGE MAP

BREEDING

YEAR-ROUND

WINTER

10s spotters

SLENDER BODY WITH SMALL HEAD

BLACK SPOTS ON WINGS

LONG, POINTED TAIL

MALE

be a BIRD NERD!

There are the same number of MOURNING DOVES living in the United States as people—about 350 million. They take up residence in open areas and backyards. These birds live long lives, averaging 10 years. One reached the ripe old age of 31!

EXPERT'S CIRCLE

DON'T BE FOOLED The Mourning Dove can be mistaken for the larger **WHITE-WINGED DOVE** (left), which is found in the southern United States and into Mexico. The White-winged Dove has white wing patches, a square-tipped tail, and a long bill that curves slightly downward.

GREATER ROADRUNNER

Geococcyx californianus LENGTH 23 in (58 cm) · HABITAT Open desert with some brush · FOOD Small mammals, insects, spiders, reptiles · VOICE Like a dove: *coo-coo-coo-coo*

THE GREATER ROADRUNNER was given its name for a good reason: It can run 18 miles an hour (29 km/h). The roadrunner only flies when absolutely necessary, but it can jump straight up to snag bats and small birds. Living in the open desert, a Greater Roadrunner does not need much water to survive. It gets moisture from its prey, which include insects, tarantulas, snakes, lizards, and small mammals. It beats the larger food items against rocks to soften them up before swallowing. The Greater Roadrunner hides its nest in low trees and cacti. It lowers its temperature at night and raises it in the morning by sunbathing.

>>> RANGE MAP

YEAR-ROUND

TRY THIS!

ARE YOU AS FAST as a Greater Roadrunner? This bird can zip along at about the speed you ride your bike when you're moving fast on a flat surface. Try running alongside a bike rider who pedals the same speed as you. Can you keep up? It's pretty hard to outrun a roadrunner!

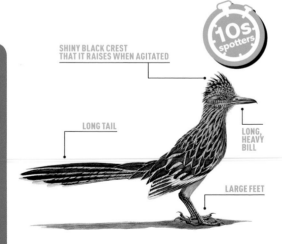

SHINY BLACK CREST THAT IT RAISES WHEN AGITATED

LONG TAIL

LONG, HEAVY BILL

LARGE FEET

10s spotters

be a BIRD NERD!

When running, GREATER ROADRUNNERS use their tail and wings as rudders—like the kind you'd find at the back of a boat—to steer.

BARN OWL

Tyto alba **LENGTH** 16 in (41 cm) • **HABITAT** Open country with trees, cliffs, buildings • **FOOD** Small mammals, rodents • **VOICE** Call is harsh, hissing screech

WITH A HEART-SHAPED white face and white breast and underwings, the Barn Owl floats like a ghostly figure through the night sky. The only sound that can be heard is its spooky hiss and raspy scream. The Barn Owl hunts only at night, using its keen vision and hearing to hunt small mammals—like rats, mice, bats, and rabbits—in open fields and meadows. It nests in holes of trees, old barn lofts, or abandoned buildings. Barn Owls sometimes store large amounts of prey at the nesting site while incubating their eggs.

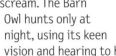

>>> RANGE MAP

BREEDING

YEAR-ROUND

10s spotters

BEIGE AND GRAY ON HEAD AND BACK

DARK EYES

HEART-SHAPED FACE

WHITE BODY, FACE, AND UNDERWINGS

be a BIRD NERD!

The **BARN OWL** has amazing hearing. Its ability to locate a mouse under the grass in complete darkness is the most accurate of any animal ever tested. With its slow, quiet wingbeats, this owl glides over fields, through the dark of night, listening for its prey. The owl's face is divided into two disks that collect the sound waves and funnel them toward its ears.

Laugh Out Loud!

What was the Barn Owl's favorite school subject?

OWLgebra!

BURROWING OWL

Athene cunicularia LENGTH **9.5 in (24 cm)** • HABITAT **Scrubby terrain, grasslands, golf courses** • FOOD **Insects, small mammals** • VOICE **A two-note *coo coooo***

BURROWING OWLS nest in holes in the ground, but they rarely do any of the digging themselves. Instead, they take over a discarded burrow of a rabbit, skunk, armadillo, or prairie dog. They primarily eat insects during the day and hunt for small mammals, like mice, at night. They live in dry, open areas, pastures, prairie dog towns, and even vacant lots. Burrowing Owls sometimes hunt by flying down from a perch, but they will also hunt by hopping or running on the ground. In the daytime, this diminutive owl can be found sitting in the entrance of its burrow, comically scowling at the world.

>>> RANGE MAP

BREEDING

YEAR-ROUND

MIGRATION

WINTER

be a BIRD NERD!

BURROWING OWLS collect the dung of other animals and spread it around the doorways and insides of their burrows. This attracts dung beetles, which they eagerly devour. It also helps control carbon dioxide levels in the air, which can make it difficult to breathe in those narrow, burrow tunnels.

ADULT

JUVENILE

SPOTS ON ITS BACK

LONG LEGS

NO STRIPES ON CHEST

10s spotters

Laugh Out Loud!

What type of books do owls like to read?

Hoooo-dunnits!

EASTERN SCREECH-OWL

Megascops asio LENGTH 8.5 in (22 cm) · HABITAT Forests, farmlands, city parks · FOOD Mice, lizards, insects, frogs, other birds · VOICE Call is an even-pitched trill and a shrill whinny

WHEN YOU'RE EAST of the Rockies and out at night, listen for the Eastern Screech-Owl, which is commonly found in woods, suburbs, and parks. Its call sounds like a horse's whinny. Eastern Screech-Owls spend their days in tree cavities and their nights searching for food, like mice and even other birds. When roosting, they strike a pose so they look like part of the tree bark or a dead stick.

>>> RANGE MAP

YEAR-ROUND

BIG HEAD, ALMOST NO NECK

EAR TUFTS OFTEN RAISED

10s spotters

ADULT RED MORPH

JUVENILE GRAY MORPH

WESTERN SCREECH-OWL

Megascops kennicottii LENGTH 8.5 in (22 cm) · HABITAT Open woodlands, urban parks, residential areas · FOOD Mammals, birds, insects, crayfish · VOICE Call is a series of short hoots

LIKE ITS EASTERN COUSIN, the Western Screech-Owl makes its presence known by its distinctive short whistles. Found west of Kansas, it is commonly seen in woodlands and deserts and nests in tree cavities, although it will readily make a backyard owl box its home. It seeks out small animals, worms, and insects for its meals.

TUFTED EARS

YELLOW EYES

ADULTS GRAY OR BROWNISH GRAY WITH STREAKED FEATHERS

10s spotters

>>> RANGE MAP

YEAR-ROUND

GREAT HORNED OWL

Bubo virginianus **LENGTH** 22 in (56 cm) • **HABITAT** Woodlands, swamps, farmland • **FOOD** Mammals, birds, reptiles, fish, insects • **VOICE** Call is deep hoots: *hoo hoo-HOO hoooo hoo*

THE GREAT HORNED OWL is one of the most common owls found in North America, living in deserts, wetlands, forests, and even cities. It is also one of the most distinctive. It has huge yellow eyes that can see in the dark, and its head is like a radar dish that can swivel 270 degrees. Its prey varies from large birds to frogs to insects and it raises its family in nests built by other birds. Its deep hoots are often set in five syllables: *hoo hoo-HOO hoooo hoo*. Great Horned Owls weigh only 3 to 4 pounds (1.3–1.8 kg), yet they can catch prey up to ten pounds (4.5 kg)—the size of a house cat. Its wing feathers have soft edges that allow it to fly in silence, like a spy plane. It also has 3-D hearing, allowing it to locate prey hiding under brush or snow, even when it's pitch-black out.

>>> RANGE MAP

YEAR-ROUND

be a BIRD NERD!

OWLS swallow their food whole. For Great Horned Owls, that can even be a small rabbit or skunk. They have also killed large prey like Great Blue Herons, but the herons are way too heavy to carry, so the owl eats only the heron's head.

"HORNS" THAT ARE ACTUALLY SOFT FEATHERS

10s. spotters

LARGE YELLOW EYES

BARREL-SHAPED BODY

SHARP TALONS FOR CATCHING PREY

EXPERT'S CIRCLE

DON'T BE FOOLED With long ear tufts that point straight up, the **LONG-EARED OWL** (left) could be mistaken for a Great Horned, but the Long-eared is about 7 inches (18 cm) smaller. There's nothing small about its hoot, though—males can be heard up to 0.7 mile (1 km) away. It also has a very distinct white X on its face.

BARRED OWL

Strix varia **LENGTH 21 in (53 cm)** • **HABITAT Mature forests, river bottoms, swamps** • **FOOD Small mammals, reptiles, birds, fish, insects** • **VOICE Call is deep hooting** *who-cooks-for-you, who-cooks-for-YOU-ALL*

BARRED OWLS are one of the most vocal owls in North America. They have brown-and-white-striped feathers and dark, soulful eyes. Barred Owls live in swamps and wet forests, and pluck fish straight from streams or ponds. They also eat small mammals, reptiles, birds, and insects. Barred Owls nest high up in trees and do not migrate. Young owls climb trees using their bill and talons to hold on.

>>> RANGE MAP

YEAR-ROUND

DARK EYES

BARRED BREAST

VERTICAL STREAKS BELOW BARRED BREAST

SPOTTED OWL

Strix occidentalis **LENGTH 18 in (46 cm)** • **HABITAT Western old-growth coniferous forests; rocky canyons** • **FOOD Small mammals, rodents** • **VOICE A call of four notes:** *hup, hoo-hoo, hoooo*

SPOTTED OWLS prefer to live and nest in old-growth forests that are at least 200 years old, which means their habitat is under threat from logging. Spotted Owls, which are dark brown with small white spots, have dark brown circles around their big brown eyes. They eat mostly flying squirrels and wood rats, and nest in tree cavities or in old raptor or squirrel nests.

ROUND HEAD WITHOUT EAR TUFTS

DARK EYES

DARK BROWN WITH SMALL WHITE SPOTS

>>> RANGE MAP

YEAR-ROUND

COMMON NIGHTHAWK

Chordeiles minor **LENGTH 9.5 in (24 cm)** · **HABITAT Woodlands, suburbs**
· **FOOD Insects** · **VOICE Call is a nasal** *peent*

NIGHTHAWK is a misleading name because the Common Nighthawk doesn't strictly hunt at night and it isn't closely related to hawks. Common Nighthawks feast on insects in the early morning or evening hours, catching their food while they fly. Then they dip low and skim water surfaces to drink. Nighthawks have a graceful, batlike quality, which earned them the nickname "Bullbats." Common Nighthawks live in rural and urban areas, including coastal sand dunes and beaches, and can often be seen flying over brightly lit baseball fields on warm summer evenings, gulping down insects. They nest on flat gravel rooftops, gravel beaches, or open forest floors.

>>> RANGE MAP

BREEDING

MIGRATION

→ LOOK FOR THIS The **COMMON NIGHTHAWK** male flies above treetops and will suddenly drop in a dive to the ground. Just before it looks like it's about to crash, it pulls up, flexing its pointed wings downward. Listen up: The rushing air across its wingtips makes a deep booming sound.

LONG POINTED WINGS WITH WHITE STRIPE, OR BAR ON OUTER HALF

10s spotters

GRAY, WHITE, BEIGE (OR BUFF), AND BLACK FEATHERS

V-SHAPED WHITE THROAT PATCH

be a BIRD NERD!

COMMON NIGHTHAWKS dart about at dawn and dusk like bats, flying with their mouths open and swallowing moths and other insects whole.

EASTERN WHIP-POOR-WILL

Antrostomus vociferus LENGTH **9.75 in (25 cm)** • HABITAT **Open forests** • FOOD **Insects** • VOICE **A repeated *whip-poor-will* call**

YOU CAN LOCATE an Eastern Whip-poor-will by its call, but seeing one is an entirely different matter. They are notoriously difficult to find. Their gray-brown feathers blend in perfectly with dead leaves on the forest floor. At night, they perch on low branches and fly off to catch moths and other insects. During the day, they roost on the ground or on a tree branch. The female Eastern Whip-poor-will nests on the ground, directly on leaves. While they aren't songbirds, their repeated call of *whip-poor-will* sounds like a song.

>>> RANGE MAP

BREEDING
MIGRATION
WINTER

OFTEN CLOSES ITS EYES WHEN PERCHED

10s spotters

LARGE ROUNDED HEAD

STOUT CHEST

be a BIRD NERD!

EASTERN WHIP-POOR-WILLS time the laying of their eggs with the cycle of the moon. On average, eggs hatch ten days before a full moon. They don't build nests, but lay two eggs directly on the forest floor. When the moon is almost full, the adults gather lots of insects to feed young babies still in the nest, called nestlings.

TRY THIS!

CURIOUS WHAT an Eastern Whip-poor-will sounds like? Check out an audio recording of its song at the Cornell Lab of Ornithology's All About Birds website: allaboutbirds.org/guide/Eastern_Whip-poor-will/sounds. Can you imagine the words "whip poor will" when you listen to it?

CHIMNEY SWIFT

Chaetura pelagica LENGTH 5.25 in (13 cm) · HABITAT Areas that have chimneys for nesting; they winter in South America · FOOD Flying insects · VOICE High-pitched *chip* call in flight

AS THEIR NAME WOULD IMPLY, Chimney Swifts nest in chimneys and on the walls of abandoned buildings. Way back, before there were chimneys, the birds would nest in hollow trees and caves. When they aren't flying to catch insects, Chimney Swifts are unable to perch on branches like other birds. Their strong claws are made to cling to walls and other vertical surfaces. They even have tiny spine-like projections at the tips of their tail feathers that help them attach to rocky walls. On fall evenings, flocks of migrating Chimney Swifts circle above church steeples or large chimneys and then dive in at high speeds to spend the night there.

>>> RANGE MAP

BREEDING

MIGRATION

10s spotters

SHORT TAIL

CIGAR-SHAPED BODY

SWEPT-BACK WINGS

TRY THIS!

CHIMNEY SWIFTS will build a home in your chimney if the chimney cap is off. Remind your parents to keep the damper closed in the spring and summer when the birds are nesting and do not light a fire until they leave in the fall.

be a BIRD NERD!

CHIMNEY SWIFTS "glue" the twigs of their nest together and stick them to the walls of chimneys using their own sticky saliva.

WHITE-THROATED SWIFT

Aeronautes saxatalis LENGTH 6.5 in (17 cm) • HABITAT Mountains, coastal cliffs, urban areas • FOOD Insects • VOICE Call is descending scraping notes

ONE OF THE FASTEST flying birds in North America, the White-throated Swift speeds through the sky hunting for flying insects. It has thin, swept-back wings and a pointed tail. Its plumage is black and white with a white stripe down its belly. It holds its long tail in a point. White-throated Swifts cruise above river gorges, coastal cliffs, and cities in pursuit of flying insects. They "glue" together the materials of their saucer-shaped nest with their own saliva. At night, White-throated Swifts sleep in roosts of hundreds, huddling together in crevices in cliffs and holes in canyon walls. When they swirl into the roost in large groups, some miss and bounce off the cliff's wall, and then rejoin the flock.

>>> RANGE MAP

BREEDING
YEAR-ROUND
MIGRATION
WINTER

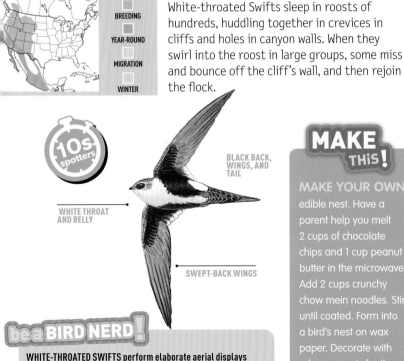

10s spotters

BLACK BACK, WINGS, AND TAIL

WHITE THROAT AND BELLY

SWEPT-BACK WINGS

bea BIRD NERD!

WHITE-THROATED SWIFTS perform elaborate aerial displays during courtship—swooping, swirling, and twirling in the sky.

MAKE THiS!

MAKE YOUR OWN edible nest. Have a parent help you melt 2 cups of chocolate chips and 1 cup peanut butter in the microwave. Add 2 cups crunchy chow mein noodles. Stir until coated. Form into a bird's nest on wax paper. Decorate with a few peanuts for the eggs. Enjoy!

RUBY-THROATED HUMMINGBIRD

Archilochus colubris LENGTH **3.75 in (10 cm)** · HABITAT **Parks, gardens, meadows, woodland edges** · FOOD **Nectar, tiny insects** · VOICE **Call is soft *tchew* notes**

RUBY-THROATED HUMMINGBIRDS, the only species of hummingbird commonly found on the East Coast, are feisty: When hovering around gardens or feeders, they are quick to chase off other hummingbirds to keep food supplies all to themselves. It takes a lot of energy for hummingbirds to beat their wings so fast, so they are constantly eating. They lap up nectar with a long tongue that has a brushy tip. They also eat small insects. Only the male Ruby-throated Hummingbird has the signature iridescent ruby red throat. Females have a white throat and a green back. Hummingbirds don't vocalize much, but you can listen for the hum of their rapidly beating wings.

>>> RANGE MAP

BREEDING
YEAR-ROUND
MIGRATION
WINTER

TRY THiS!

TRY FLAPPING your arms like a HUMMINGBIRD flaps its wings. Move your arms like you're drawing the number eight with your fingertips. How many eights can you do in one second? How many seconds does it take you to do 75?

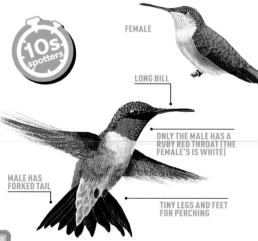

10s. spotters

FEMALE

LONG BILL

ONLY THE MALE HAS A RUBY RED THROAT (THE FEMALE'S IS WHITE)

MALE HAS FORKED TAIL

TINY LEGS AND FEET FOR PERCHING

be a BIRD NERD!

HUMMINGBIRDS can beat their wings in a figure-eight motion at a rate of 75 times per second!

ANNA'S HUMMINGBIRD

Calypte anna LENGTH 4 in (10 cm) · HABITAT Urban and suburban areas, open woodlands · FOOD Nectar, tiny insects · VOICE Call is sharp *chit* notes

ANNA'S HUMMINGBIRD is the most common hummingbird on the Pacific Coast. Found in gardens and around feeders, it eats nectar as its main source of food. Males have an iridescent red throat and crown. When courting, a male hovers in front of a female. It flies straight up in the air—up to ten stories high—then plummets down and pulls out of the dive inches before reaching the female.

>>> RANGE MAP

BREEDING

YEAR-ROUND

WINTER

MALES: RED THROAT AND CROWN

10s spotters

BROAD TAIL

BROAD-TAILED HUMMINGBIRD

Selasphorus platycercus LENGTH 4 in (10 cm) · HABITAT Open woodlands and meadows · FOOD Nectar · VOICE Call is metallic chips

BROAD-TAILED HUMMINGBIRDS nest high in the Rocky Mountains. Their main source of food is nectar from wildflowers. Males have a red throat, while females have a white throat with green spots. Both have broad tails. It can get cold in the Rockies, and a Broad-tailed Hummingbird can go into a state called torpor: It lowers its body temperature and slows its heart rate to conserve energy.

10s spotters

BROAD TAIL

MALE: RED THROAT

FEMALE: THROAT IS WHITE WITH GREEN SPOTS

>>> RANGE MAP

BREEDING

YEAR-ROUND

MIGRATION

WINTER

RUFOUS HUMMINGBIRD

Selasphorus rufus LENGTH **3.75 in (10 cm)** • HABITAT **Open woodlands, meadows, swamps, parks, backyards** • FOOD **Nectar, insects, spiders** • VOICE **A sharp *tewk* call**

RUFOUS HUMMINGBIRDS are small, but they are fierce! They will fight off other hummingbirds at a feeder even when they are outnumbered and outsized. They'll even chase off a small chipmunk—which can be ten times its weight or more! "Rufous" is an English word from the 1700s meaning the color of rust or reddish brown. Male Rufous Hummingbirds are rust-colored on the top with a reddish orange throat. Females (above left) have a white throat with green and red spots and are beige-colored on their sides. These tiny birds can be found in open forests and meadows, but also at backyard feeders. Rufous Hummingbirds breed in Alaska—the farthest north of any hummingbird.

>>> RANGE MAP

BREEDING

MIGRATION

WINTER

be a BIRD NERD!

THE RUFOUS HUMMINGBIRD migrates 3,900 miles (3,276 km) from Mexico to Alaska, going up the Pacific coast and back down the Rocky Mountains. It is one of the longest journeys of any bird in relation to its body size. At just under 4 inches (10 cm) long, that's equal to flying more than 78 million body lengths!

10S spotters

RUFOUS (REDDISH) BACK

MALES: DARK RED THROAT

Laugh Out Loud!

Why do hummingbirds hum?

Because they don't know the words to the song!

BELTED KINGFISHER

Megaceryle alcyon **LENGTH 13 in (33 cm)** • **HABITAT Streams, rivers, ponds, lakes, coastal areas** • **FOOD Mostly fish; crayfish, frogs, insects** • **VOICE Call is a loud, sharp rattle**

THE BELTED KINGFISHER lives up to its name—it is a royal expert at catching fish! This bird studies the water from its perch high in a tree and when it spies a fish, it dives headfirst into the water and grabs it. Then it slams the fish against a branch to kill it and swallows it whole. Parents teach young birds how to fish by dropping dead fish in the water for them to practice on. The Belted Kingfisher knows how to show other birds who's the boss. When excited or threatened it raises the crest of feathers on its big head, spreads its wings, and strikes a pose that shows off its large, pointed bill.

>>> RANGE MAP

☐ BREEDING
☐ YEAR-ROUND
☐ WINTER

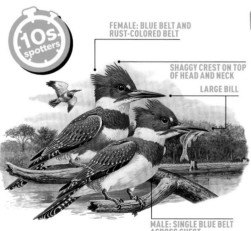

10s spotters

FEMALE: BLUE BELT AND RUST-COLORED BELT

SHAGGY CREST ON TOP OF HEAD AND NECK

LARGE BILL

MALE: SINGLE BLUE BELT ACROSS CHEST

be a BIRD NERD!

BELTED KINGFISHERS are very territorial. This ragged-crested bird will defend an area of water—not land—chasing other kingfishers away from its turf. It is generally about a half-mile (0.8-km)-long stretch of river or lakeshore. The Belted Kingfisher flies quickly up and down the shoreline giving a loud, rattling call.

→ **LOOK FOR THIS** The **BELTED KINGFISHER** is one of the few species of birds where the female is more colorful than the male. The male has a blue-and-white belt around its body; the female has two—one blue and one rust-colored. The female also digs the tunnel where they nest.

Wilson's Storm-Petrel

Oceanites oceanicus

LENGTH: 7.25 in (18 cm)
EATS: Small fish, crustaceans
VOICE: Long, grating call

Sooty Shearwater

Puffinus griseus

LENGTH: 18 in (46 cm)
EATS: Fish, crustaceans, squid
VOICE: *Coo-roo-ah* call

Black-footed Albatross

Phoebastria nigripes

LENGTH: 32 in (81 cm)
EATS: Fish, fish eggs, squid, crustaceans
VOICE: Nasal braying call
BE A BIRD NERD: The Black-footed Albatross uses its exceptional sense of smell to find food over the expanse of ocean water.

SOME BIRDS are at home over the great open ocean. When it isn't nesting in the Hawaiian Islands, the Black-footed Albatross wanders across the northern Pacific. The Wilson's Storm-Petrel is the most common bird off the Atlantic Coast of the United States. The Sooty Shearwater is the socialite of the sea, sometimes gathering in groups of hundreds of thousands, resting on rafts in the water. Both the Wilson's Storm-Petrel and the Sooty Shearwater nest in the Southern Hemisphere but fly to North America when their winter arrives.

ACORN WOODPECKER

Melanerpes formicivorus **LENGTH 9 in (23 cm)** • **HABITAT Near trees—in forests, backyards, city parks** • **FOOD Acorns, other nuts; also fruits, tree sap** • **VOICE A loud *wakka*, usually repeated**

ACORN WOODPECKERS enjoy family time. They live in colonies that may include aunts and uncles, as well as brothers, sisters, mom, and dad. They all work together to create a large store of their favorite food—acorns, natch!—in a tree or telephone pole. This woodpecker is common in the western United States wherever oak trees are abundant. You might think that the Muppet character Fozzie Bear invented the phrase *wakka wakka wakka*, but it's actually the call of the Acorn Woodpecker. The bird's call and behavior, in addition to its comical face, inspired the cartoon character Woody Woodpecker.

>>> RANGE MAP

YEAR-ROUND

→ LOOK FOR THIS

If you find a tree or telephone pole with lots of acorns pushed into it, you probably have found an **ACORN WOODPECKER** warehouse. These birds are known to store thousands of acorns in a single tree, which is known as a granary. To attach an acorn, the woodpecker first pecks a perfect acorn-size hole in a thick tree trunk. Then it inserts the nut, pounding it in firmly with its bill. Acorn Woodpecker colonies use the same granary tree year after year, making it easy to find their next meal.

FEMALE HAS BLACK FOREHEAD BAR

CLOWNLIKE FACE WITH RED CAP AND WHITE EYES

GLOSSY BLACK BACK, WHITE PATCHES ON WING AND RUMP

STIFF BLACK TAIL FEATHERS

10s spotters

Laugh Out Loud!

What do you get if you cross a parrot with a woodpecker?

A bird that talks in Morse code.

GILA WOODPECKER

Melanerpes uropygialis LENGTH **9.25 in (24 cm)** • HABITAT **Cactus and scrub deserts, towns, streamside woods** • FOOD **Insects, cactus fruits, berries** • VOICE **Rolling *churr*; also loud *yip***

THE ZEBRA-STRIPED back of a Gila Woodpecker is a little out of place in the hot desert. Nesting in tall saguaro cacti, these tan birds with a black-and-white barred back are found in the U.S. Southwest and Mexico. In this area, their color is unique among woodpeckers, so you can't miss them. They eat insects, along with cactus fruits, mistletoe berries, and even the sugary water in hummingbird feeders.

RED CROWN IN MALE

BARRED BACK

BARRED CENTRAL TAIL FEATHERS

>>> RANGE MAP

YEAR-ROUND

RED-BELLIED WOODPECKER

Melanerpes carolinus LENGTH **9.25 in (24 cm)** • HABITAT **Open woodlands, suburban trees** • FOOD **Insects, nuts, fruits, suet at feeders** • VOICE **A loud, rolling *churr***

ITS NAME MAY BE "Red-bellied," but what really shows up on the Red-bellied Woodpecker is the bright red on the head and black-and-white barred back. Its reddish pink lower belly is often difficult to spot. Year-round residents of woodlands and suburban areas, Red-bellies take advantage of the offerings at bird feeders. They sometimes take over the nests of other birds.

RED CROWN AND NAPE ON MALE, RED NAPE ON FEMALE

BLACK-AND-WHITE BARRED BACK

BARRED CENTRAL TAIL FEATHERS

>>> RANGE MAP

YEAR-ROUND

WINTER

DOWNY WOODPECKER

Picoides pubescens LENGTH 6.75 (17 cm) • HABITAT Woodlands
• FOOD Insects, bird feeder seeds, and suet • VOICE Sharp, high-pitched *pik,*
softer than a Hairy Woodpecker's

NAMED FOR THE SOFT FEATHERS on its lower back, the Downy Woodpecker shows up regularly at backyard feeders and is especially fond of suet, or beef fat. In winter, Downies hang out in mixed flocks with chickadees, nuthatches, and other small songbirds. They also drill into wood for insects and will follow the large Pileated Woodpecker, feeding off its leftovers.

MALE HAS RED CROWN

SMALL BILL

BARRED OUTER TAIL FEATHERS

FEMALE

>>> RANGE MAP

YEAR-ROUND

HAIRY WOODPECKER

Picoides villosus LENGTH 9.25 in (24 cm) • HABITAT Forests with medium to large trees • food Insects, fruits, seeds • VOICE A sharp *peek,* and also a slurred whinny

THE HAIRY WOODPECKER looks a lot like the Downy, but it is several inches longer. Otherwise, it's pretty tricky to spot the differences. The Hairy Woodpecker has a longer bill—about the length of its head—and its outer tail feathers are entirely white. It lives in open and dense forests in most of the same range as the Downy Woodpecker. It eats insects, but also fruits and seeds.

MALE HAS RED PATCH ON BACK OF HEAD

LONG, STRAIGHT BILL, ABOUT LENGTH OF HEAD

>>> RANGE MAP

YEAR-ROUND

WINTER

NORTHERN FLICKER

Colaptes auratus LENGTH 12.5 in (32 cm) · HABITAT Woodlands, suburban areas · FOOD Mostly insects, some fruits and seeds · VOICE A loud, single *klee-yer*

YOU'RE AS LIKELY TO SPOT a Northern Flicker on the ground as in a tree. These large, brown woodpeckers forage, or hunt, on the ground for insects, and may run short distances. They also feed in trees in woodlands and suburban areas. Flickers that eat a lot of ants will develop a strong taste of the formic acid that ant bodies contain—but their predators, such as hawks, don't mind.

>>> RANGE MAP

BREEDING
YEAR-ROUND
WINTER

Flickers make their nests in tree cavities, as other woodpeckers do. The call they make at breeding time is a long, loud series of *wick-er* notes. In the eastern part of their range, Northern Flickers have yellow shafts on their underwing feathers and in the western part they have red shafts.

EASTERN MALE HAS RED ON NAPE

EASTERN MALE HAS BLACK "WHISKER"

SPOTTED UNDERPARTS WITH BLACK "BIB"

WESTERN MALE HAS RED "WHISKER"

WESTERN MALE HAS NO RED ON NAPE

[FEMALES LACK "WHISKER"]

10s spotters

TRY THIS!

NORTHERN

FLICKERS drum on objects to communicate. Grab a friend and make up your own bird code by drumming on the sides of a tree with your hands. Don't talk! Can you understand each other?

be a BIRD NERD!

NORTHERN FLICKERS are regular ant-eaters! They dig for ants with their bills in the dirt or in a rotten log, then use their long, barbed tongues to lap them up. Yum!

PILEATED WOODPECKER

Dryocopus pileatus LENGTH 16.5 in (42 cm) • HABITAT Mature forests, cypress swamps • FOOD Carpenter ants, insect larvae, fruits, nuts • VOICE A single *wuck* note, or a series

THE LARGEST WOODPECKER in North America, the Pileated Woodpecker is the size of a crow. It makes a very loud drumming sound when it uses its chisel-like bill to dig into a tree or fallen log looking for insect larvae or ants—or when a male sends a territorial signal. Pileated Woodpeckers live throughout eastern North America and the Pacific Northwest, but they are most common in the Southeast. Both the male and female have a distinctive red crest, but the male's is bigger.

>>> RANGE MAP

YEAR-ROUND

be a BIRD NERD!

PILEATED WOODPECKERS nest in large, dead trees. They use their strong bills to excavate long rectangular or oval holes. They also drill large areas in the trees they feed on and have even been known to split small trees in half. Pileateds and other woodpeckers may drill on house siding—not a popular move with homeowners!

BOTH MALE AND FEMALE HAVE RED CREST, BUT MALE'S EXTENDS TO THE BILL

FEMALE

FEMALE HAS A BLACK "WHISKER" MARK; MALE'S "WHISKER" IS RED

10 S. spotters

MOSTLY BLACK WITH WHITE WING PATCHES

Laugh Out Loud!

What is a woodpecker's favorite kind of joke?

A knock-knock joke!

MONK PARAKEET

Myiopsitta monachus LENGTH **11.5 in (29 cm)** • HABITAT **Florida;
also some cities in U.S. Northeast and Midwest** • FOOD **Fruits, seeds**
• VOICE **Loud, grating** *krii*

PARAKEETS that live in cities? Yes! Monk
Parakeets are native to South America,
but they are able to stand the freezing
temperatures of cities as far north as
Chicago and New York. Some of these urban
birds were pets that escaped or were set free
and then formed
colonies in the wild. A member of the parrot
family, Monk Parakeets build large, untidy,
stick nests in trees, on buildings, and on
power poles and power stations. When they
gather in large flocks of 30 to 50, their
combined squawks can get your attention!

>>> RANGE MAP

YEAR-ROUND

THICK
PARROT
BEAK

BACK IS BRIGHT GREEN

GRAY FOREHEAD,
THROAT, AND
BREAST

WINGS LOOK
BLUISH IN
FLIGHT

10s
spotters

be a BIRD NERD!

MONK PARAKEETS build
large, messy nests using
thousands of sticks. A
single nest can be home to
a dozen or more families
that will use it year-round
for shelter. The parakeets
sometimes share their
nests with other animals,
including American Kes-
trels, Great Horned Owls,
and even opossums!

Laugh
Out Loud!

What's orange and sounds like a parrot?

A carrot!

EASTERN PHOEBE

Sayornis phoebe LENGTH **7 in (18 cm)** ▪ HABITAT **Wooded areas, often near buildings** ▪ FOOD **Flying insects** ▪ VOICE **Males sing a harsh *fee-bee*, accented on first syllable**

EASTERN PHOEBES are commonly seen flycatchers, a group of birds that—you guessed it!—catches and eats flies and other flying insects. These phoebes are common in woods, farmlands, and suburbs of eastern North America. They often build nests around human-built structures and like them to be sheltered by overhangs, such as eaves and rafters. They create their nests out of mud, moss, grasses, leaves, and other handy materials, such as spiderwebs. Eastern Phoebes perch in trees and on fence lines, bobbing their tails as they look out for flying insects. They will also eat small fruits and seeds. These birds get their name from the male's distinctive *fee-bee* call.

>>> RANGE MAP

BREEDING

YEAR-ROUND

MIGRATION

WINTER

TRY THIS!

YOU CAN encourage Eastern Phoebes to nest around your house by building a nesting ledge. Get an adult to download free instructions from a website that shows how to build birdhouses and nesting platforms. Then get help making and mounting it where the birds will be safe from cats and squirrels.

SHORT, THIN BILL

DARK BROWN ABOVE

PALE YELLOW BELLY IN FALL, WHITISH IN SPRING

10s spotters

be a BIRD NERD!

Bird observers once thought that phoebes were devoted to one mate. (Seems they got it wrong!) DNA studies reveal that a male may pair with two females and that the eggs in one nest may have more than one father.

BLACK PHOEBE

Sayornis nigricans LENGTH **6.75 in (17 cm)** ∘ HABITAT **Western North America, almost always near water** ∘ FOOD **Mostly insects, but occasionally small minnows** ∘ VOICE **Males sing a repeated *tee-hee tee-hoo***

THE BLACK PHOEBE is the only black-and-white flycatcher in North America. Its "outfit" resembles a black shirt and white pants! It catches flying insects on the wing. The Black Phoebe doesn't mind living near people as long as it's near water, including swimming pools. They build nests from mud and plant fibers against natural and human-made structures, like roof eaves.

>>> RANGE MAP

BREEDING

YEAR-ROUND

WINTER

STRAIGHT, THIN BILL

MOSTLY BLACK, WHITE ON BELLY AND UNDER TAIL

SAY'S PHOEBE

Sayornis saya LENGTH **7.5 in (19 cm)** ∘ HABITAT **Open country, canyons, deserts, foothills** ∘ FOOD **Flying insects** ∘ VOICE **A fast *pit-tse-ar***

FROM NORTH TO SOUTH, the Say's Phoebe has a longer nesting range than any other flycatcher in North America. It nests from Alaska to the southern tip of California and south into Mexico. This grayish brown bird lives in dry foothills, canyons, deserts, and badlands. It builds nests on cliff ledges and buildings. The Say's catches insects in flight, but also hovers over vegetation to snag a snack.

GRAYISH BROWN BACK

BELLY IS CINNAMON-COLORED

>>> RANGE MAP

BREEDING

YEAR-ROUND

MIGRATION

WINTER

VERMILION FLYCATCHER

Pyrocephalus rubinus **LENGTH 6 in (15 cm)** ∙ **HABITAT Scrub, desert, woodlands** ∙ **FOOD Insects** ∙ **VOICE A sharp, thin** *pseep*

SMALL AND SHARPLY DRESSED in eye-catching red with a blackish brown mask and upperparts, the male Vermilion Flycatcher can't be missed. The female is much less noticeable, with grayish brown upperparts and streaked-white underparts. She also has a little peachy pink on the belly and under the tail. Vermilion Flycatchers live in the desert and in woodlands and often are found near streams and ponds. They build their nests in trees, fashioning them from twigs and grasses and lining them with feathers. They spend much of their time perched and on the lookout for insects.

>>> RANGE MAP

☐ BREEDING
☐ YEAR-ROUND
☐ WINTER

TRY THIS!

THE WORD "VERMILION" describes a shade of red that really pops out. The vibrant color attracts the ladies. Try going on a walk and identifying other colors in nature. Make a list and choose your favorite.

MALE HAS A BLACKISH MASK

FEMALE HAS PEACHY PINK ON LOWER BELLY AND UNDER TAIL

MALE HAS BRIGHT RED BODY WITH DARK UPPERPARTS

be a **BIRD NERD!**

The male **VERMILION FLYCATCHER** pumps up the drama during breeding season. He performs a spectacular courtship display that begins with an ascent to about 50 feet (15 m) above the trees. He sings at the top of his lungs as he descends in a flutter to perch in a tree. He repeats this multiple times and may even present a potential mate with a colorful butterfly!

WESTERN KINGBIRD

Tyrannus verticalis LENGTH 8.75 in (22 cm) • HABITAT Open areas with scattered trees, farms, ranches • FOOD Flying insects • VOICE Fussy sputtering and also *kip* notes

THE WESTERN KINGBIRD'S range continues to expand, thanks to the planting of trees and installation of utility poles on the Great Plains. These provide more perches and nesting spots for this active and entertaining bird, known for dive-bombing much larger birds such as ravens and hawks. This kingbird's pale gray body sports a bright, lemony yellow belly. It eats insects, catching them in mid-flight.

>>> RANGE MAP

BREEDING

MIGRATION

WINTER

PALE GRAY HEAD AND BACK

YELLOW BELLY

WHITE-EDGED TAIL

10s spotters

EASTERN KINGBIRD

Tyrannus tyrannus LENGTH 8.5 in (21 cm) • HABITAT Open areas with scattered trees, orchards, parks • FOOD Flying insects • VOICE Harsh *dzeet* note, often in series

DESPITE ITS NAME, the Eastern Kingbird occurs as far west as Oregon, Washington, and British Columbia. It can be found in open fields, along forest edges, and even on golf courses. This small territorial bird has a lot of feisty confidence and will chase away much larger predatory birds, such as eagles. These kingbirds eat insects in summer and tropical fruits in winter.

BLACKISH HEAD

WHITE TAIL TIP

10s spotters

>>> RANGE MAP

BREEDING

MIGRATION

SCISSOR-TAILED FLYCATCHER

Tyrannus forficatus LENGTH 13 in (33 cm) • HABITAT Grasslands,
prairies • FOOD Insects, especially grasshoppers, crickets, beetles
• VOICE Fussy sputtering and *pup* notes

NO WONDER Oklahoma chose the
Scissor-tailed Flycatcher as its state bird.
Anyone who has seen this amazing bird in
flight, scissoring its spectacular tail as it
turns, will ever forget it. Then there's the
happy fact that the bird's small breeding range
is centered in Oklahoma. Scissor-tailed Flycatchers migrate between this area and Central
America in late fall and early spring. Before
migrating south in the fall, the flycatchers
often roost in flocks of up to 1,000 birds. At
other times, they sit out in the open on fences
and other perches, scoping out insects in flight
or on the ground.

>>> RANGE MAP

BREEDING
MIGRATION
WINTER

be a BIRD NERD!

Just flying around in its daily
life, the male SCISSOR-TAILED
FLYCATCHER is a very impressive bird. But in the spring
males put on courtship displays
that wow and amaze. They
take off on extended flights,
wheeling and dipping in the air.
This dazzles the females—and
human observers!

10s spotters

PALE GRAY HEAD
AND BACK

YOUNG BIRDS
HAVE MUCH
SHORTER
TAILS

LONG BLACK-AND-WHITE TAIL

PINKISH BELLY

→ **LOOK FOR THIS** In the air, male and female **SCISSOR-TAILED FLYCATCHERS** can look quite alike. They have
similar plumage, but the male's tail tends to be noticeably longer. Young flycatchers overall are paler than their parents
and have shorter tails.

LOGGERHEAD SHRIKE

Lanius ludovicianus LENGTH **9 in (23 cm)** · HABITAT **Open country with scattered bushes** · FOOD **Large insects, lizards, mice, other birds** · VOICE **Harsh** *shack-shack*

WITH THE NICKNAME "butcher birds," you can guess that shrikes aren't warm-and-fuzzy types. This songbird has the hooked bill of a predator and uses it to grab and kill prey. Then it carries the prey in its bill and impales it on a thorn. Sometimes a shrike will eat its meal on the spot. Often, it's saved for later, although stored food is at risk of being raided by other birds. Shrikes burn up a lot of energy and must eat frequently. Loggerhead Shrikes prefer open country with low shrubs to perch on. There they wait and watch, swooping down on an insect, lizard, small bird, or mouse.

>>> RANGE MAP

BREEDING

YEAR-ROUND

WINTER

True **or** False

Q: "Loggerhead" is another word for "blockhead."

A: TRUE! Loggerhead Shrikes have an unusually large head in relation to the size of their body.

Q: Loggerhead Shrikes refuse to hunt if it's too cold outside.

A: FALSE! In fact, they use the cold to their advantage: When other animals are slowed down by the cold, Loggerheads strike!

BLACK MASK

HOOKED BILL

10s. spotters

PLUMAGE IS GRAY, BLACK, AND WHITE

The **LOGGERHEAD SHRIKE** lacks talons—sharp claws—so it goes after its prey with its sharp bill. Grabbing the intended victim with the bill, the shrike kills with a bite to the neck.

BIRDTASTICS:
Birds With Strange Behaviors

Florida Scrub-Jay

Aphelocoma coerulescens
LENGTH: 11 in (28 cm)
EATS: Acorns, small invertebrates
VOICE: Call has raspy, hoarse notes

Common Poorwill

Phalaenoptilus nuttallii
LENGTH: 7.75 in (20 cm)
EATS: Night-flying insects
VOICE: Song is a whistled *poor-will*

BIRDS CAN have some pretty quirky habits. To get females to notice him, the male Greater Sage-Grouse creates a noise using the air sacs on his chest that sounds like a rock plopping into the water. Then there's the Common Poorwill, one of a few birds that hibernate in winter. Its metabolic rate slows and its body temperature drops. It may stay that way for several weeks. Florida Scrub-Jays have very strong family ties—last year's young stay home and help their parents raise nestlings.

Greater Sage-Grouse

Centrocercus urophasianus

LENGTH: 28 in (71 cm) male; 22 in (56 cm) female
EATS: Plants, flowers, fruits, insects
VOICE: During display, air sacs make loud popping call
LIFE SPAN: 7 years
BE A BIRD NERD: When a Greater Sage-Grouse wants to attract a female, it inflates and deflates air sacs otherwise hidden under feathers.

ON THE SAGEBRUSH PLAINS OF THE WEST, A GREATER SAGE-GROUSE USES AN OPEN AREA, CALLED A LEK, TO DISPLAY TO A FEMALE.

BLUE JAY

Cyanocitta cristata LENGTH **11 in (28 cm)** · HABITAT **Woodlands, parks, suburbs** · FOOD **Nuts, seeds, fruits, insects, worms** · VOICE **A loud, squawking** *jay-jay-jay*

WHEN THEY'RE OUT AND ABOUT, Blue Jays get noticed. Their colorful plumage, proud crests, loud, squawking calls, and bossy behavior can't be ignored. They thrive on acorns, which they can carry in a special throat pouch, and eat other seeds, fruits, and insects. When Blue Jays find too many acorns to eat in one sitting, they bury them under leaves in the woods. Blue Jay nestlings demand a high-protein diet—and parents provide it by feeding them nestlings of other bird species. Jays will also eat other birds' eggs. And they love the offerings at bird feeders, often hogging the food until they have had their fill.

>>> RANGE MAP

- [ ] BREEDING
- [ ] YEAR-ROUND
- [ ] WINTER

Laugh Out Loud!

What bird is always sad?

A Blue Jay!

be a BIRD NERD!

BLUE JAYS' sounds range from a quiet *wheedle-wheedle* to their loud signature call: *jay-jay-jay*. Blue Jays often mimic the scream of the Red-shouldered Hawk, causing people to search the sky for it!

CREST

10s spotters

WHITE TIPS ON BLUE WINGS

BLACKISH "NECKLACE"

LONG TAIL FEATHERS WITH WHITE TIPS

→ **LOOK FOR THIS** You can tell a lot about how a **BLUE JAY** feels by looking at its crest. When chillin' in the nest, its crest is usually flattened. When threatened or feeling aggressive, the crest is fully raised.

STELLER'S JAY

Cyanocitta stelleri LENGTH 11.5 in (29 cm) ▪ HABITAT Pine-oak woodlands, coniferous woodlands ▪ FOOD Nuts, seeds, berries, insects ▪ VOICE A piercing *sheck-sheck-sheck*

BOTH MALE AND FEMALE Steller's Jays show a handsome color combo of turquoise, dark blue, and black, along with a shaggy crest. Being jays, they are smart and resourceful. Steller's jays know how to grab a meal from western campers and hikers by pickpocketing or even pulling bacon off grills! They also eat nuts, fruits, and insects, and they often visit backyard bird feeders.

LONG BLACK CREST

DARK BLUE WINGS WITH BLACK BARRING

>>> RANGE MAP

YEAR-ROUND

WINTER

WESTERN SCRUB-JAY

Aphelocoma californica LENGTH 11 in (28 cm) ▪ HABITAT Brushy areas, open woods, parks, suburbs ▪ FOOD Nuts, seeds, fruits, insects, lizards ▪ VOICE Upslurred *jaaay?* or *jreee?*

SMART AND SNEAKY, Western Scrub-Jays look for ways to score an easy meal or gain an advantage. One will spy on another jay to see where it hides food so it can come back later and steal it. Suspicious scrub-jays also look around for thieves before they stash food. The birds are territorial in nesting season, but they hang in flocks in winter.

BLUE HEAD WITH WHITE EYEBROW

SHORT WINGS AND LONG TAIL

HEAVY BLACK BILL

>>> RANGE MAP

YEAR-ROUND

WINTER

AMERICAN CROW

Corvus brachyrhynchos LENGTH 17.5 in (45 cm) · HABITAT Wide variety, including open areas with scattered trees · FOOD Grain, insects, small animals, carrion, garbage · VOICE Harsh *caw-caw-caw-caw*

THE AMERICAN CROW is a familiar large black bird that often is seen in flocks, especially in fall and winter. These very social birds live throughout the United States and much of Canada in a wide variety of habitats. American Crow families consist of as many as 15 individuals and the species is very community-minded. Researchers have observed a crow mom taking over the care of a neighbor's young orphaned during a virus epidemic. Crows are smart and highly adaptable—and not too picky about the condition of their food! They often fly over streets and highways searching for roadkill. Squashed squirrel seems to be a favorite.

>>> RANGE MAP

BREEDING
YEAR-ROUND
WINTER

be a BIRD NERD!

The old-fashioned term "as the crow flies" comes from the fact that CROWS tend to fly in a straight line, taking the most direct routes to a destination (without having to use GPS). Humans usually have to rely on paths and roads that wind and turn, so crow "mileage" isn't a very useful measure for us!

10s spotters

GLOSSY BLACK FEATHERS

HEAVY BLACK BILL

MALES AND FEMALES LOOK IDENTICAL

EXPERT'S CIRCLE

DON'T BE FOOLED In the eastern U.S., especially in the Southeast, there are two types of crows, the American Crow and the FISH CROW. They look very similar, but one way to tell them apart is by sound. The American caws, while the Fish Crow makes a high, nasal *uh, uh*.

COMMON RAVEN

Corvus corax LENGTH 24 in (61 cm) • HABITAT Mountains, desert, coastal areas, grasslands • FOOD Grain, insects, small animals, carrion, garbage • VOICE Croaking *kraaah* and a hollow *brooonk*

RAVENS ARE AMONG the smartest animals on Earth. They are capable of using sticks as tools and they understand some basic forms of cause and effect. The can even solve multiple-step problems using these abilities. For thousands of years, ravens have lived in close association with humans and are at home in both the natural and man-made worlds. The Common Raven resembles the American Crow, although it's almost 50 percent larger, has shaggy neck feathers, and has a heavier bill than the crow. The Common Raven is more common in western North America than in its eastern range. It has been adopted as the provincial bird of Canada's Yukon Territory.

>>> RANGE MAP

YEAR-ROUND

WINTER

BILL HEAVIER THAN AMERICAN CROW'S

SHAGGY THROAT FEATHERS

WEDGE-SHAPED TAIL

10s spotters

True **or** False

Q: Captive ravens are kept at the Tower of London.

A: TRUE! Legend has it that the British Empire will crumble if there aren't six ravens kept as residents at the Tower of London.

. . . .

Q: Ravens are capable of mimicking human sounds.

A: TRUE! Some captive ravens have been taught to mimic human words just like parrots.

be a BIRD NERD!

RAVENS like to play games in flight, performing rolls and somersaults in midair.

HORNED LARK

Eremophila alpestris LENGTH **7 in (18 cm)** • HABITAT **Open country; prefers bare ground** • FOOD **Seeds; feeds insects to young** • VOICE **Call is a high *tsee-ee***

HORNED LARKS are widespread songbirds known for their distinctive "horns," or tufts of black feathers on top of the head. They can be found on dry, bare ground, in places like deserts, tundra, prairies, beaches, and grazed pastures. The female builds a nest directly on the ground, weaving it out of grasses or other plant materials. Horned Lark populations have declined steeply in the past 50 years, perhaps due to housing development and the loss of farmland. Larks are especially musical in the mornings, singing a series of sharp, high-pitched tinkling notes.

>>> RANGE MAP

- [ ] BREEDING
- [ ] YEAR-ROUND
- [ ] MIGRATION
- [ ] WINTER

→ **LOOK FOR THIS** Watch for a chance to observe the **HORNED LARK'S** spectacular sky dance. In spring, a male Horned Lark conspicuously defends its nesting territory by making a very dramatic flight-song display. He flies straight up into the sky in silence to a height of up to 800 feet (244 m), where he breaks into his high-pitched flight song. He hovers and circles while singing. When finished, he pauses—and drops headfirst steeply toward the ground. At the last moment, he stops before he hits bottom. Awesome!

10s spotters

TWO BLACK "HORNS" FORMED BY FEATHER TUFTS

FACE AND THROAT ARE WHITE OR YELLOW

BLACK MASK AND BIB

Female **HORNED LARKS** often collect pebbles and corncobs and place them next to their nests, creating a kind of walkway.

PURPLE MARTIN

Progne subis LENGTH **8 in (20 cm)** • HABITAT **Fields, meadows, parks, streams, dunes** • FOOD **Flying insects** • VOICE **Loud gurgling and whistles; also** *churr* **call**

NORTH AMERICA'S LARGEST SWALLOW,

the Purple Martin looks like its tiny bill might keep it from getting enough insects to survive. But look closer: Its mouth opens to reveal a cavern! Martins eat most types of flying insects, from large dragonflies to tiny midges. Western birds tend to nest in natural cavities, such as woodpecker holes. Eastern birds nest in hollowed-out gourds (a tradition begun by Native Americans) placed in groups for their convenience and also in multifamily birdhouses, which may have 20 separate "apartments." During migrations to and from the Amazon Basin, where they winter, martins often roost together by the thousands.

>>> RANGE MAP

BREEDING

MIGRATION

be a BIRD NERD!

PURPLE MARTINS that live in the East almost exclusively nest in birdhouses. Western ones almost always use natural cavities.

FEMALES ARE DULLER, WITH GRAY ON THE HEAD AND CHEST

MALES ARE DEEP PURPLE OVERALL WITH BROWN-BLACK WINGS AND TAIL

TRY THIS!

PURPLE MARTINS eat crushed eggshells to help them digest their food. Put some eggshells outside your window to try to see some Purple Martins up close!

TREE SWALLOW

Tachycineta bicolor LENGTH 5.75 in (15 cm) • HABITAT Marshes, open fields • FOOD Insects, berries • VOICE Calls and song include whistles and liquid gurgles

MALE TREE SWALLOWS are hard to miss—they have an iridescent deep blue-green back and white chest. (Females have more brown and are duller.) They feast on flying insects, but also plants and berries in fall and winter. They prefer to live near water, where the insects are plentiful. Tree Swallows nest in old woodpecker holes or birdhouses. They are social and migrate in huge flocks.

>>> RANGE MAP

BREEDING

YEAR-ROUND

MIGRATION

WINTER

MALE: BRIGHT BLUE BACK AND WHITE CHEST

LONG, POINTED WINGS

CLIFF SWALLOW

Petrochelidon pyrrhonota LENGTH 5.5 in (18 cm) • HABITAT Open areas with overhanging cliffs or structures like bridges • FOOD Flying insects • VOICE Song consists of subdued squeaks and twitters; call a low-pitched *churr*

CLIFF SWALLOWS don't just hang around cliffs—they also live in canyons and river valleys. In summer, these birds nest under bridges and overpasses. Flying insects like mayflies, moths, and bees are their main food. Cliff Swallows build nests in tightly packed colonies of up to 3,000 birds. They collect mud to build a gourd-shaped nest and line it with dry grass.

WHITE FOREHEAD

DARK BLUE BACK

REDDISH BROWN THROAT

>>> RANGE MAP

BREEDING

MIGRATION

BARN SWALLOW

Hirundo rustica **LENGTH 6.75 in (17 cm)** • **HABITAT** Fields, pastures, golf courses • **FOOD** Flying insects • **VOICE** Song is a series of squeaky warbles; call a high-pitched *chee-jit*

THE MOST ABUNDANT swallow in the world, the Barn Swallow has a long, forked tail and a slender body. This bird is graceful enough to easily swoop in and out of a barn door to its nest. Barn Swallows hunt for flying insects—like bees, butterflies, and wasps—often just a few inches above the ground and over water. Besides in barns, they build their nests under bridges and the eaves of roofs. Barn Swallows can be seen swooping over ball fields, open fields, lakes, and beaches. They have a range from sea level up to 10,000 feet (3,050 m).

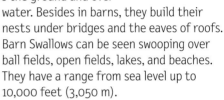

>>> RANGE MAP

BREEDING

YEAR-ROUND

MIGRATION

WINTER

LONG, FORKED TAIL

BUFF BELLY

10s spotters

REDDISH THROAT

ADULTS

GLOSSY BLUE BACK

TRY THiS!

WANT TO INVITE a Barn Swallow into your barn or outbuilding? Open a door or window and leave mud and straw nearby that it can use to build its nest. The swallow will line its nest with dry grass.

BARN SWALLOW parents sometimes use "nest helpers" to feed their young. They are usually older siblings who bring insects to the baby birds.

TUFTED TITMOUSE

Baeolophus bicolor **LENGTH 6.25 in (16 cm)** • **HABITAT Forests, orchards, parks** • **FOOD Insects, seeds, nuts, berries** • **VOICE Song is whistled *peter peter peter;* call a harsh *zhee zhee zhee***

THE TUFTED TITMOUSE gets its name from its tall crest, or tuft. This bird also has a black forehead and large black eyes. Tufted Titmice live in forests and suburbs in the eastern United States, nesting in cavities and birdhouses. The birds line their nest with soft fur, which they pluck from the tails of road-killed squirrels and sleeping raccoons! They eat mostly insects, but also seeds, nuts, and berries. A young titmouse will often help its parents raise the next generation of birds. Their song can be heard in woodsy backyards throughout the East and is a cheerful *peter peter peter* repeated up to 11 times.

>>> RANGE MAP

YEAR-ROUND

TRY THIS!

WANT TO ATTRACT Tufted Titmice to your backyard? Lure them with their favorite snacks! Try stocking a bird feeder with black oil sunflower seeds, mealworms, peanuts, or suet—they're not picky.

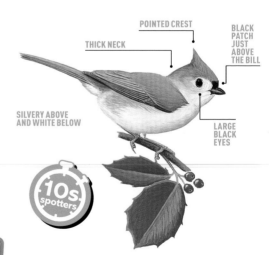

POINTED CREST

THICK NECK

BLACK PATCH JUST ABOVE THE BILL

SILVERY ABOVE AND WHITE BELOW

LARGE BLACK EYES

10s spotters

be a BIRD NERD!

TUFTED TITMICE are hoarders! In fall and winter, they gather sunflower seeds and other birdseed one at a time from backyard feeders. They store the seeds up to 130 feet (40 m) away from the feeder.

BLACK-CAPPED CHICKADEE

Poecile atricapillus LENGTH 5.25 in (13 cm) • HABITAT Woodlands, willow thickets, suburbs • FOOD Insects, seeds, berries • VOICE Song is a clear, whistled *fee-bee;* call a slow *chick-a-dee-dee-dee*

BLACK-CAPPED CHICKADEES are friendly—they're often the first to discover a new bird feeder and are comfortable coming right up to a window. They are found in forests, parks, thickets, and backyards. They eat seeds, berries, and plant matter, but also insects, spiders, and suet. They nest in cavities and nest boxes. Black-capped Chickadees are curious and social. Flocks may have calls to alert one another. They make a *chick-a-dee-dee-dee* call and use an increasing number of *dee* notes when they are alarmed. This friendly little bird weighs less than half an ounce (14 g).

>>> RANGE MAP

YEAR-ROUND

WINTER

10s. spotters

OVERSIZE ROUND HEAD

BLACK CAP AND BIB

GRAY BACK

WHITE CHEEKS

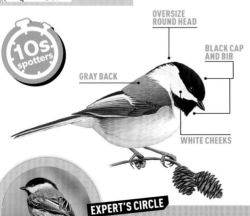

be a **BIRD NERD!**

The BLACK-CAPPED CHICKADEE hides seeds—each in a different place. Unlike a human, it can remember thousands of hiding places. This acrobat is able to hang upside down by its feet. It can also be tamed—with lots of patience—to feed from your hand.

EXPERT'S CIRCLE

DON'T BE FOOLED CAROLINA CHICKADEES (left) and Black-capped Chickadees are almost identical, except the edges of the Black-capped's wing feathers are lined in bright white in the fall and winter. The Carolina's are edged in a light gray color. Carolina Chickadees can be found all over the southeastern United States—from the Atlantic coast to Oklahoma. The Black-capped Chickadee seems immune to cold, snowy weather and can be found as far north as Alaska in the United States, and New Brunswick, Canada.

WHITE-BREASTED NUTHATCH

Sitta carolinensis LENGTH **5.75 in (15 cm)** • HABITAT **Mature forests, parks, backyards** • FOOD **Insects, seeds, nuts** • VOICE **Song is series of whistles on one pitch; call is nasal** *yank*

LOOK CAREFULLY around tree trunks—if you see a bird creeping on the bark upside down, it may be a White-breasted Nuthatch. This bird is nimble at climbing up and down tree bark. White-breasted Nuthatches live in mature forests and wooded backyards. Their main source of food is insects, like larvae, ants, and caterpillars, but they also eat seeds and nuts, including acorns and sunflower seeds. They are attracted to backyard feeders with sunflowers, peanuts, and suet. They build their nests in cavities or abandoned woodpecker holes, lining them with fur or bark. Their call is a loud, low-pitched nasal *yank*. The song is a series of whistles on one pitch. The calls of birds in the Rockies and on the West Coast are higher pitched.

>>> RANGE MAP

YEAR-ROUND

WINTER

→ LOOK FOR THIS
WHITE-BREASTED NUT-HATCHES were given their name because they shove large nuts and acorns into the bark of trees and whack at them with their dagger-like bill until the seed "hatches." Then they eat the meaty kernel inside. If you spot a nuthatch near a tree, look carefully to see if you can spot it "hatching" a nut!

These agile little birds aren't picky eaters. They also like beetles, spiders, and bugs, and have a very clever way to find them. The nuthatches move headfirst down a tree, which allows them to see the insects hiding in the bark's crevices that other birds, like woodpeckers, don't see because they are moving upward.

SHORT TAIL

10s spotters

BLUE-GRAY ON THE BACK WITH WHITE FACE AND UNDERPARTS

LARGE HEAD

be a **BIRD NERD!**

NUTHATCHES have an extra-long hind claw that can grip tree bark in any position.

RED-BREASTED NUTHATCH

Sitta canadensis LENGTH 4.5 in (11 cm) • HABITAT Mountain forests • FOOD Insects, spiders, seeds • VOICE Song is rapid series of *ehn ehn ehns;* call is nasal *ehhnk, ehhnk* that sounds like a toy horn

RED-BREASTED NUTHATCHES live in fir and spruce forests, where they dig their own nest cavities, usually in dead branches or tree trunks. They can take up to 18 days to complete. In the summer, they eat mostly insects and other arthropods, like beetles, spiders, ants, and earwigs. In the winter, they eat seeds from conifer trees. They will also eat peanuts, sunflower seeds, and suet from backyard feeders. Red-breasted Nuthatches can be aggressive— especially at feeders. They sometimes stock up on seeds, storing them in bark for lean times in the winter.

>>> RANGE MAP

BREEDING

YEAR-ROUND

WINTER

10 S. spotters

SHORT TAIL

GRAY CAP AND BACK

CINNAMON UNDERPARTS, WHICH ARE PALER IN FEMALES

BLACK EYE LINE

be a BIRD NERD!

RED-BREASTED NUTHATCHES are tiny, but they are bold. They will do anything to create a good nest—even steal. They sometimes sneak nest-lining materials, like animal fur, strips of bark, and feathers, from the nests of other nuthatches or chickadees. Then they usually lay five to six eggs, which hatch 12 to 13 days later.

→ **LOOK FOR THIS** For tight security from enemies, **RED-BREASTED NUTHATCHES** drill their own hole in a tree. Then they collect sticky globs of resin from fir, pine, and hemlock trees and smear it around the entrance to their nest hole. The male smears it on the outside and the female on the inside. The resin is placed there to keep predators out—but it doesn't keep the nuthatch from flying in. Red-breasted Nuthatches dive straight into their nest hole without getting all gummed up!

BIRDTASTICS:
Rio Grande Valley Birds

Great Kiskadee

Pitangus sulphuratus
LENGTH: 9.75 in (25 cm)
EATS: Insects, spiders, lizards, mice
VOICE: Call is *kis-ka-dee*

THE RIO GRANDE VALLEY in southern Texas is a subtropical region that is a haven for almost 500 species of birds. Some neotropical birds found nowhere else in the United States— like the Green Jay, Great Kiskadee, and Plain Chachalaca—live there year-round. Other species come to breed and nest, and then return to their winter homes in Mexico and Central and South America. Some from the North only live there in the winter.

GREEN JAYS PERCH IN TEXAS BRUSH AND WOODLANDS.

Green Jay

Cyanocorax yncas

LENGTH: 10.5 in (27 cm)
EATS: Arthropods, invertebrates, seeds
VOICE: Raspy *cheh-cheh-cheh* call
BE A BIRD NERD: The Green Jay is a tropical bird, and its colors show it: From below the neck it's all green. It has a black chest and bright blue face.

Plain Chachalaca

Ortalis vetula

LENGTH: 22 in (56 cm)
EATS: Buds, berries, insects
VOICE: Call is *cha-cha-lac*

HOUSE WREN

Troglodytes aedon LENGTH 4.75 in (12 cm) • HABITAT Open woods, thickets, backyards • FOOD Insects, spiders • VOICE Song is cascade of whistled notes; calls include a soft *chek* and harsh scold

HOUSE WRENS are easy birds to have around your backyard—they are attracted to birdhouses and eat a variety of insect pests. They have even been seen feeding insects to chicks of other species. They aren't always the good guys, though. Sometimes House Wrens peck or remove the eggs and nestlings of other nesters, such as bluebirds and chickadees, especially if those birds are occupying a nest site that they want. (Nest holes and nest boxes can be hard to find!) House Wrens live in open woods and thickets. Besides insects, they also eat spiders. Both males and females sing. During breeding season, males sing 9 to 11 times per minute.

>>> RANGE MAP

- ☐ BREEDING
- ☐ YEAR-ROUND
- ☐ MIGRATION
- ☐ WINTER

MAKE THiS!

A HOUSE WREN will often make a nest in a birdhouse that is firmly attached to a building, pole, or tree around your home. It should be 5 to 10 feet (1.5–3 m) above the ground. The right size birdhouse is important: 5.5 inches by 5.5 inches (14 by 14 cm), with a 1-inch (2.5-cm) entry hole, is good. You can find instructions on a birding website.

CURVED BEAK

SHORT WINGS

BROWN OVERALL WITH DARK BARRING ON THE WINGS

10s spotters

be a BIRD NERD!

HOUSE WRENS sometimes add spider egg cases to their nests. Why? When the spiderlings hatch, they eat the mites on the baby wrens.

CAROLINA WREN

Thryothorus ludovicianus LENGTH 5.5 in (14 cm) ▪ HABITAT Woods, ravines, backyards ▪ FOOD Insects, spiders ▪ VOICE Call is a cheer and chattering sounds

IF YOU'RE IN THE WOODS in the eastern United States during summer, you'll likely hear the rolling song of a Carolina Wren— *tea-kettle, tea-kettle, tea-kettle!* Only the male belts out this loud three-part song.

Reddish brown, the Carolina Wren has a noticeable white eyebrow stripe and curved bill. Its tail is usually cocked up, but it is lowered when it sings. Carolina Wrens live in shrubby wooded areas, overgrown farmland, and brushy yards. They nest in open cavities, and in any container they can find.

>>> RANGE MAP

YEAR-ROUND

LONG WHITE EYEBROW STRIPE

WHITE CHIN AND THROAT

REDDISH BROWN UPPERPARTS

10s spotters

True or False

Q: The Carolina Wren will nest in old shoes, mailboxes, and flowerpots.

A: TRUE! They nest in crevices and cavities of just about anything! They'll even try to nest in pockets of coats on a clothesline!

Q: Both male and female Carolina Wrens belt out loud songs.

A: FALSE! The male Carolina Wren is the only one that sings loudly.

be a BIRD NERD!

This wren sings loudly year-round. Observers once recorded the songs of a CAROLINA WREN in captivity. It sang nearly 3,000 times in a single day.

MARSH WREN

Cistothorus palustris LENGTH 5 in (13 cm) · HABITAT Marshes, especially with dense reeds · FOOD Insects, spiders · VOICE Song is a mix of bubbling and trilling notes; call a sharp *tsuk*

AS YOU MIGHT EXPECT from its name, the Marsh Wren seeks out marshland for its habitat. This bird is usually found in and around reeds and cattails. It looks for food near the marsh floor, and finds insects on plants or in the water. Marsh Wrens build a football-shaped nest made of grasses and plants that has a side entrance. These noisy birds sing all day and into the night.

>>> RANGE MAP

BREEDING

YEAR-ROUND

MIGRATION

WINTER

MOSTLY BROWN WITH A DARK CAP

TAIL IS OFTEN UPRIGHT

WHITE EYEBROW STRIPE

10s spotters

CACTUS WREN

Campylorhynchus brunneicapillus LENGTH 8.5 in (22 cm) · HABITAT Desert cacti · FOOD Insects, spiders · VOICE Song is *char char char char char char char*; call is low, croaking notes

THE LARGEST WREN in North America, the Cactus Wren lives in the cactus-filled deserts of the Southwest. It doesn't need to spend time looking for water—it gets its liquids from the insects it eats and from biting juicy cactus fruits. The insects it eats include beetles, ants, wasps, and grasshoppers. They eat spiders, too. They make their nests in the arms of cholla cacti.

10s spotters

BOLD WHITE EYEBROW STRIPE

STREAKS AND BARS ON WINGS

SPOTTED BREAST

>>> RANGE MAP

YEAR-ROUND

BLUE-GRAY GNATCATCHER

Polioptila caerulea LENGTH **4.25 in (11 cm)** • HABITAT **Woodlands, thickets** • FOOD **Insects, spiders** • VOICE **Song is series of thin, wiry notes; call a whining *pweee***

DESPITE THE Blue-gray Gnatcatcher's name, gnats do not make up a significant amount of its diet. These birds eat plant bugs, tree bugs, leaf beetles, weevils, and spiders. Blue-gray Gnatcatchers live in a variety of woodland habitats, from chaparral to mature forests. In the northern part of their range, they nest along rivers, streams, and lakes. Males and females work together for several weeks to build a cuplike nest, which is held together and attached to a tree branch with spider webbing. This nest of spider silk can stretch as the chicks grow. Constantly in motion, the Blue-gray Gnatcatcher has a wheezy, rambling song.

>>> RANGE MAP

- BREEDING
- YEAR-ROUND
- MIGRATION
- WINTER

BLUE-GRAY WITH WHITISH UNDERPARTS

STRAIGHT BILL

LONG TAIL

BREEDING MALE

LONG LEGS

10s spotters

MAKE THiS!

BUILD A gnatcatcher nest. Turn over a cereal bowl and cover it in plastic wrap. In another bowl, mix 3 ounces (89 mL) of glue and 3 ounces (89 mL) of water. Cut 8-inch (20-cm)-long strips of construction paper (a half inch [1.3 cm] wide), dip them in glue, and press them to the wrap until it's covered. After 24 hours, remove your dried nest.

be a BIRD NERD!

The **BLUE-GRAY GNATCATCHER'S** coloring and the way it imitates other birds' sounds has earned it the nickname "little mocking jay."

AMERICAN DIPPER

Cinclus mexicanus LENGTH 7.5 in (19 cm) • HABITAT Mountain and coastal streams • FOOD Aquatic insects, larvae, minnows • VOICE Long, ringing series of musical notes

AMERICAN DIPPERS aren't afraid of a little cold—even freezing—water. Their bodies are built for cold temperatures, with thick plumage, a low metabolic rate, and blood that can carry a lot of oxygen. Standing on a wet rock in an icy river, a dipper will jump in and walk underwater in search of food. Its name, "Dipper," comes from its unusual way of "dipping," or plunging under the water to catch the food. Fighting the currents, it snags insect larvae and also catches small minnows. Dippers nest in crevices or on ledges or under overhanging dirt banks along streams. The constant spray of chilly water doesn't seem to hurt the dippers or their chicks.

>>> RANGE MAP

☐ YEAR-ROUND
☐ WINTER

True **or** False

Q: The American Dipper's nickname is Chilly Dipper.

A: FALSE! It's "water ouzel." An ouzel is a bird that resembles a blackbird.

. . . .

Q: Sometimes, the American Dipper is flightless.

A: TRUE! Unlike most songbirds, the American Dipper molts its wing and tail feathers all at once in late summer, which makes it flightless for a period of time.

HEAVY, ROUNDED BODY, SOOTY GRAY WITH SHORT TAIL

DARK BILL

be a BIRD NERD!

AMERICAN DIPPERS are never far from water—they'll even build their nests behind a small waterfall!

RUBY-CROWNED KINGLET

Regulus calendula LENGTH **4.25 in (11 cm)** • HABITAT **Coniferous forests, mixed woods, brushy habitats** • FOOD **Insects, spiders** • VOICE **Husky, scolding** *je-dit*

RUBY-CROWNED KINGLETS are constantly on the move, flicking their wings as they dart through the forest in search of insects and spiders. These small birds do things in a big way. The male's song is exceptionally loud for his size. The female lays the largest clutch, or group of eggs, for a small North American songbird—up to 12 at a time. That's a lot of eggs for a tiny bird to keep warm. She layers them in the nest and probably uses her legs as well as her brood patch (bare belly skin) to do the job.

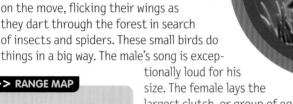

>>> RANGE MAP

BREEDING
YEAR-ROUND
MIGRATION
WINTER

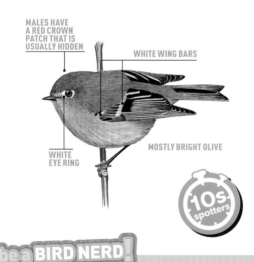

MALES HAVE A RED CROWN PATCH THAT IS USUALLY HIDDEN

WHITE WING BARS

MOSTLY BRIGHT OLIVE

WHITE EYE RING

10S spotters

be a BIRD NERD!

When feeding, RUBY-CROWNED KINGLETS seldom stay in one spot for more than one or two seconds, and are constantly flicking their wings. When a male is upset at another male or trying to impress a female, he raises the feathers on his head to show off his red crown.

TRY THIS!

HERE'S A MATH problem for you: A Ruby-crowned Kinglet weighs about the same as its clutch of eggs. If a Ruby-crowned Kinglet weighs 0.4 ounce (11.3 g) and she lays 12 eggs, how much does each of her eggs weigh?

. . . .

Answer: 0.033 ounce (0.9 g) (less than the weight of half a dime!)

AMERICAN ROBIN

Turdus migratorius **LENGTH 10 in (25 cm)** • **HABITAT Wooded areas, open fields, urban areas** • **FOOD Earthworms, fruits, berries** • **VOICE Loud, musical** *cheerily cheer-up cheerio*

FEW PEOPLE in North America wouldn't recognize an American Robin. The familiar bird hops through lawns hunting the worms it loves to eat. It stands motionless with its head cocked to the side, picking up a worm vibe. In the blink of an eye, the worm goes "down the hatch!" When European settlers first saw the bird, they named it for one they knew from home that's unrelated to this one. Many robins stay put in winter, feeding on berries and fruits. They may gather in huge flocks of up to a quarter million birds. As spring approaches, the males sing and the birds build nests on shrubs, trees, and man-made structures. Robins usually have two clutches of eggs a year. The father tends to the first batch of fledglings while the mother re-nests with the second.

>>> RANGE MAP

BREEDING
YEAR-ROUND
WINTER

be a BIRD NERD!

ROBINS aren't shy. They sometimes build their nests in porch eaves, on outdoor lights, or even on a window-sill. Nests that are low to the ground often fall prey to outdoor cats and other predators.

→ LOOK FOR THIS

Many people associate the **AMERICAN ROBIN'S** song with the beginning of spring. You'll quickly recognize its cheery melody: a string of ten or more clear whistles. To hear it any time of year, you can search its call on the Web, but be sure an adult helps you!

WHITE CRESCENTS AROUND THE EYE

YELLOW BILL

BRICK RED UNDERPARTS

STRONG LEGS

EASTERN BLUEBIRD

Sialia sialis LENGTH 7 in (18 cm) • HABITAT Open country: pastures, farm fields, parks • FOOD Insects, berries, other small fruits • VOICE Rich, musical *chur chur-lee chur-lee*

PEOPLE WHO PUT UP backyard birdhouses with the hope of attracting Eastern Bluebirds often are disappointed, unless the yard borders some kind of field. These birds like open country—you're more likely to see one on a summer road trip. Check out birds perching on utility lines. Male Eastern Bluebirds have a royal blue back and head and reddish breast. Females are similar, but grayer.

DEEP BLUE UPPERPARTS

MALE

REDDISH BROWN BREAST

FEMALE GRAYER, PALER

>>> RANGE MAP

BREEDING

YEAR-ROUND

WINTER

WESTERN BLUEBIRD

Sialia mexicana LENGTH 7 in (18 cm) • HABITAT Open woodlands • FOOD Insects, spiders, snails • VOICE Call is a single *few*; song a series of *few* notes

THE MALE Western Bluebird is more purplish blue than the Eastern, with a solid-blue head. These birds live in open woodlands in the western United States and Canada. They nest in tree cavities that occur naturally or are dug by stronger-billed birds, such as woodpeckers. A male can get very territorial in the breeding season and "wrestle" a rival, pinning him to the ground.

MALE

PURPLE-BLUE ABOVE

BREAST AND SIDES CHESTNUT

FEMALE IS BROWNISH GRAY ABOVE, PALER UNDERNEATH

>>> RANGE MAP

BREEDING

YEAR-ROUND

MIGRATION

WINTER

HERMIT THRUSH

Catharus guttatus LENGTH 6.75 in (17 cm) • HABITAT Coniferous or mixed woodlands, thickets • FOOD Insects, small fruits • VOICE Song a series of clear, flutelike notes

AS ITS NAME SUGGESTS, the Hermit Thrush isn't a very flashy or outgoing bird. Its brownish plumage with a spotted breast helps it stay hidden in the forest understory, where it looks for insects. But the Hermit Thrush is one of the first birds to arrive in its breeding areas, announcing its presence with an extremely sweet and beautiful song. Hermit Thrushes nest near or on the ground, often beneath conifers or shrubs.

>>> RANGE MAP

- BREEDING
- YEAR-ROUND
- MIGRATION
- WINTER

BROWNISH ABOVE
SPOTTED BREAST
REDDISH TAIL
10s spotters

....

WOOD THRUSH

Hylocichla mustelina LENGTH 7.75 in (20 cm) • HABITAT Deciduous and mixed woods • FOOD Insects, other leaf-litter invertebrates • VOICE Complex song, middle phrase is *ee-oh-lay*

THE SHY Wood Thrush searches eastern woodlands for insects and other invertebrates that live in the leaf litter. This thrush blends well with its surroundings until it stands upright, revealing a white breast spotted with black. A loud, haunting song also gives away its location. Cowbirds often knock Wood Thrush eggs out of the nest and replace them with their own.

BOLD WHITE EYE RING
REDDISH BROWN ABOVE
10s spotters

>>> RANGE MAP

- BREEDING
- MIGRATION
- WINTER

NORTHERN MOCKINGBIRD

Mimus polyglottos LENGTH **10 in (25 cm)** ▪ HABITAT **Thickets, brushy areas** ▪ FOOD **Insects, small fruits** ▪ VOICE **Original and mimicked phrases, repeated two to six times**

IF IT'S LATE at night and you hear a bird singing, chances are it's a Northern Mockingbird. Males without mates sometimes sing all night, hoping to improve their chances of finding a companion. A Northern Mockingbird continues to add to its song collection throughout its lifetime. It incorporates the songs of other birds as well as imitating other animals—including humans—other natural sounds, and even mechanical sounds. This performance, called mimicry or mocking, often takes place from a perch where it can easily be seen by others. Northern Mockingbirds are busy breeders, raising as many as four broods, or litters of young, in a year.

>>> RANGE MAP

BREEDING

YEAR-ROUND

WINTER

10s spotters

YELLOW EYES

MOSTLY GRAY ABOVE

WHITE PATCHES ON WINGS

OUTER TAIL FEATHERS WHITE

be a BIRD NERD!

When a NORTHERN MOCKING-BIRD is searching for a meal in the grass, it sometimes opens its wings wide in a series of jerks. Scientists think this may cause the insects to startle and reveal their presence. It may also be that the Northern Mockingbird is telling other birds to stay away from its feast. Maybe it doesn't like to share!

Laugh Out Loud!

What do you call a bird that likes to tease?

A mocking bird!

GRAY CATBIRD

Dumetella carolinensis LENGTH **8.5 in (22 cm)** •
HABITAT **Thickets, brushy forest, tangled vines** • FOOD **Insects,
small fruit** • VOICE **A harsh, catlike** *mew*

MEOW, Y'ALL! The Gray Catbird, a year-round resident in the southeastern states, gets its name from the sound of its main call, a harsh, catlike *mew*. It also sings a jumbled song of a mixture of melodious, nasal, and squeaky notes and is a good mimic of other birdsongs. Catbirds live in thickets, brushy areas, and amid tangled vines, where they build their nests. They may stay hidden in the brush, darting out cautiously to catch insects—or to make raids into a fruit or vegetable patch. Gardeners complain that catbirds eat their berries and poke random holes in tomatoes on the vine with their sharp, slender bills. Gray Catbirds often act out against other birds, destroying the nests and nestlings of their neighbors, including sparrows.

>>> RANGE MAP

BREEDING
YEAR-ROUND
MIGRATION
WINTER

TRY THIS!

GRAY CATBIRDS spend a lot of time keeping themselves hidden from view. You may be able to get one to make an appearance by doing what bird-watchers do: Make a repeated "pishing" sound—that is, keep saying *pish pish pish pish*. Before long, a curious catbird will likely come to investigate.

BLACKISH TAIL

STEEL GRAY OVERALL

BLACKISH CAP

CHESTNUT PATCH UNDER TAIL

10S spotters

BROWN THRASHER

Toxostoma rufum LENGTH **11.5 in (29 cm)** • HABITAT **Thickets, woodlands, forest edges** • FOOD **Insects, other invertebrates, fruits, seeds** • VOICE **A series of repeated melodious phrases**

IF YOU'RE LOOKING for a Brown Thrasher, look down on the ground. This bird spends a lot of its time walking or hopping around, finding food. It picks through leaves, its long, thin bill hunting for everything from beetles to caterpillars to lizards to tree frogs. In spring, a male may sing an extensive playlist of 1,000 songs! These birds nest low in shrubs or on the ground. Young are feathered and ready to leave home in only nine days.

RANGE MAP

BREEDING

YEAR-ROUND

MIGRATION

WINTER

REDDISH ABOVE

YELLOW EYES

LONG TAIL

10s spotters

CURVE-BILLED THRASHER

Toxostoma curvirostre LENGTH **11 in (28 cm)** • HABITAT **Arid brushland, cactus-rich deserts** • FOOD **Insects, seeds, cactus fruits** • VOICE **Call a sharp *whit-wheet***

THE MOST COMMON THRASHER in the Southwest, the Curve-billed Thrasher uses its namesake bill to search through dead plants or poke holes in soil while it's looking for insects. The Curve-billed sings a lot of elaborate songs, but not as many as a mockingbird or Brown Thrasher. The Curve-billed builds a cup-shaped nest out of thorny twigs, often on a cholla cactus or spiny shrub.

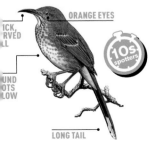

ORANGE EYES

ICK, RVED LL

UND OTS LOW

LONG TAIL

10s spotters

>>> RANGE MAP

YEAR-ROUND

BIRDTASTICS:
Beautiful Birds

Painted Bunting

Passerina ciris

LENGTH: 5.5 in (14 cm)
EATS: Seeds, insects, spiders
VOICE: Loud, rich *chip* call
BE A BIRD NERD: The French name for Painted Bunting is *nonpareil*, meaning "without equal."

LIKE A RAINBOW, A PAINTED BUNTING BRIGHTENS ITS BRUSH-FILLED HABITAT.

Elegant Trogon

Trogon elegans

LENGTH: 12.5 in (32 cm)
EATS: Insects, fruits
VOICE: Call has hoarse, croaking notes

Golden-winged Warbler

Vermivora chrysoptera

LENGTH: 4.75 in (12 cm)
EATS: Insects, spiders
VOICE: Dry, sharp *chip* call

ALL BIRDS HAVE a certain something, but some—like these three—appear to have flown right out of a fairy tale. The plumage of the male Painted Bunting represents a painter's palette, with blue, red, green, and yellow plumage more beautiful than a rainbow. The male Elegant Trogon is also a showstopper, with its coppery green upperparts and red underparts separated by a white band. The eye-catching male Golden-winged Warbler wears crisp gray, black, and white, accented with bright yellow, including a yellow crown fit for a king. Have you noticed? In the bird world, it's mainly males that get the fancy feathers.

EUROPEAN STARLING

Sturnus vulgaris LENGTH 8.5 in (22 cm) • HABITAT Lawns, fields, trees, around buildings • FOOD Insects, berries, seeds • VOICE Song has squeaks, warbles, chips, and twittering

BEFORE 1890, there weren't any European Starlings in North America. Today, there are 200 million. This invasive species, imported by European immigrants, is aggressive. It pushes native birds—like woodpeckers, blue-birds, and titmice—out of their nest holes. But when the sun hits them right and you can see their glossy green-purple plumage shine, they are birds to appreciate. European Starlings copy the songs of other birds and make their own mix of rattles and buzzes. They aren't picky eaters—they eat insects, spiders, earthworms, and also fruits, berries, and seeds. They live where people do—around houses and parks.

>>> RANGE MAP

☐ BREEDING
☐ YEAR-ROUND

be a BIRD NERD!

In 1890 and 1891, a total of 100 STARLINGS from Europe were released in New York City's Central Park. A group of people wanted to introduce every bird mentioned by Shakespeare. It took only about half a century for these adaptable birds to spread from coast to coast.

10s spotters

GLOSSY GREEN-AND-PURPLE FEATHERS THAT ARE SPOTTED WITH WHITE IN FALL AND WINTER

SHORT TAIL AND POINTED WINGS

POINTED BILL (YELLOW IN SUMMER AND BLACK IN WINTER)

→ **LOOK FOR THIS** A flock of **STARLINGS** is called a murmuration—and once you've seen one you'll never forget it. The flock flies like a giant cloud that morphs to a new shape when the birds change direction or speed.

CEDAR WAXWING

Bombycilla cedrorum LENGTH **7.25 in (18 cm)** • HABITAT **Deciduous, coniferous, and mixed woodlands, often near streams** • FOOD **Berries, other fruits, some insects** • VOICE **Soft, high-pitched, whistled** *zeee*

OFTEN HEARD before they are seen because of their high-pitched calls, Cedar Waxwings love their berries. The live in various types of woodlands and eat berries (and other fruits) almost all year round. In the winter, you can find them feasting on the cedar berries that give them part of their name. The other part—"waxwing"—comes from the waxy red tips of the wing feathers that are found mostly on older birds. The waxwing is a very attractive bird, from the tip of its pert crest to the bright yellow tip of its tail. Female Cedar Waxwings weave cup-shaped nests from grasses, twigs, horsehair, and other found materials. These birds sometimes don't nest until fall, when there is an abundance of fruits available.

>>> RANGE MAP

BREEDING

YEAR-ROUND

WINTER

CREST THAT OFTEN LIES FLAT

10s spotters

PALE BROWN HEAD WITH BLACK "BANDIT" MASK

OLDER BIRDS HAVE WAXY RED WINGTIPS

BRIGHT YELLOW TAIL TIP

be a BIRD NERD!

CEDAR WAXWINGS will pass a petal or berry from bird to bird until one finally eats it. As each one presses down on the food, it becomes a little softer. This might be a way of "prepping" it, especially a tough-skinned berry, to make it more digestible. Cedar Waxwings love the fruits of dogwoods, junipers, hawthorns, and—you guessed it—cedars!

→ **LOOK FOR THIS** Most **CEDAR WAXWINGS** have a distinctive yellow tail tip, but in the 1960s, some with orange tail tips began showing up in the northeastern United States. The orange comes from the red pigment found in the berries of an introduced species of honeysuckle. If waxwings are eating a lot of these berries while growing their tail feathers, the tips will be orange instead of yellow. What color is the tail tip on the Cedar Waxwings that you find? If it's orange, you'll have a pretty good idea of their eating habits!

COMMON YELLOWTHROAT

Geothlypis trichas **LENGTH** 5 in (13 cm) • **HABITAT** Marshes, fields, shrubs • **FOOD** Insects, spiders • **VOICE** Loud, rolling song: *wichity wichity wichity wich;* call a raspy *tschep*

WHO WAS THAT masked warbler? It's the Common Yellowthroat, known also for his bright yellow throat and chest. Though small and shy, he has a big voice. If you happen to catch one singing from a high perch, it's guaranteed to make your day! Male Yellowthroats sometimes feed their mates, and both parents feed their nestlings. Nests are usually located on or near the ground, around cattails, grasses, and grasslike sedges. When chicks fledge—develop the feathers they need to fly—females may leave the nest to start another brood.

>>> RANGE MAP

BREEDING

YEAR-ROUND

MIGRATION

WINTER

TRY THIS!

YOU CAN MAKE a difference in our understanding of warbler migration and bird behavior in general by joining a citizen science effort. One way to do this is to go on the website eBird (with adult supervision, of course) to report any bird you see. Your observations go into a database used by scientists and conservationists!

MALES HAVE A BROAD BLACK MASK AND YELLOW THROAT AND BREAST

FEMALES LACK THE MASK, ARE OLIVE GREEN ABOVE AND PALE YELLOW BELOW

10s spotters

be a BIRD NERD!

Like other songbirds that migrate at night, **COMMON YELLOWTHROATS** call while flying in the dark, probably to help keep a safe distance from others.

YELLOW WARBLER

Setophaga petechia LENGTH 5 in (13 cm) • HABITAT Willows and thickets along rivers, streams, marshes • FOOD Insects • VOICE Song is rapid *sweet sweet sweet I'm so sweet*

IF YOU SEE A brilliant yellow shape flitting across your backyard, it could be a male Yellow Warbler. (Females aren't quite as bright.) Living in thickets along streams and wetlands, Yellow Warblers are often seen darting among willows. They also live at higher elevations. Yellow Warblers eat mostly insects that they pick off of vegetation or while hovering over plants. They build their nest in the fork of a bush or small tree. Predators of Yellow Warbler nests include garter snakes, jays, crows, skunks, and cats. Males sing a series of six to ten notes over the course of a one-second song.

>>> RANGE MAP

BREEDING

YEAR-ROUND

MIGRATION

WINTER

STRAIGHT, THIN BILL

LARGE BLACK EYES

MALES ARE EGG-YOLK YELLOW WITH REDDISH STREAKS ON THE UNDER-PARTS

FEMALES AREN'T AS BRIGHT AND HAVE FAINT STREAKS

→ **LOOK FOR THIS** A sneaky female **BROWN-HEADED COWBIRD** may pull a trick on a Yellow Warbler known as nest parasitism (that means living off the Yellow Warbler's nest and her hard work as a mother). At nesting time the cowbird may slip into a Yellow Warbler's nest and lay her own egg. A cowbird's eggs are much bigger than a warbler's eggs. The female warbler is too tiny to push the big, unwanted egg out of her nest, so she seals off the nest and builds another one on top of it. If the cowbird mother comes again to lay her egg, the warbler mother builds another nest on top of the new one. Some nests have been discovered with six levels!

be a BIRD NERD!

Tiny YELLOW WARBLERS are small enough that they sometimes get caught in the webs of orb weaver spiders.

YELLOW-RUMPED WARBLER

Setophaga coronata LENGTH 5.5 in (14 cm) • HABITAT Coniferous and mixed woodlands • FOOD Insects, berries • VOICE Song is a slow warble

AS YOU MIGHT EXPECT, Yellow-rumped Warblers have yellow rumps—and also some yellow on their sides. In summer, they live in open coniferous forests. In the fall, they move south and live in more open woods and shrubby areas, and even in urban parks. Yellow-rumped Warblers glean insects from leaves, sometimes snagging them while hovering. Conifer branches are their favorite nesting place. Yellow-rumps living in the North and East have white throats and are known as Myrtle Warblers. Those in the West have yellow throats and are called Audubon's Warblers.

>>> RANGE MAP

☐ BREEDING
☐ YEAR-ROUND
☐ MIGRATION
☐ WINTER

→ LOOK FOR THIS

Timing is everything when you're trying to get a good look at a **YELLOW-RUMPED WARBLER.** Like a lot of other birds, these warblers wear some very subdued colors in winter. In preparation for the spring breeding season, the warblers molt—they change their plumage by losing old feathers. Their fresh plumage reveals a mix of eye-catching bright yellow, charcoal, and black and white.

MALE MYRTLE WARBLER

YELLOW RUMP

SIDE PATCHES THAT ALMOST DISAPPEAR IN THE FALL

MALE AUDUBON'S WARBLER

be a BIRD NERD!

The YELLOW-RUMPED WARBLER has a gut that can handle the digestion of waxy bayberries and other tough berries that grow abundantly in eastern coastal areas as far north as New England. By wintering in these locations—farther north than other warblers—Yellow-rumps can arrive in nesting areas earlier in the spring and have less competition.

EASTERN TOWHEE

Pipilo erythrophthalmus **LENGTH 7.5 in (19 cm)** • **HABITAT** Tangles, thickets, overgrown fields • **FOOD** Insects, seeds, berries • **VOICE** Song sounds like *drink your tea*; call is an upslurred *towhee*

THE EASTERN TOWHEE is an oversize sparrow that, as its name suggests, lives in the eastern United States. To spot one, look down! It eats, sings, and roosts at eye level or below, scratching the ground and moving debris with its feet as it moves along the ground with a two-footed hop. The Eastern Towhee forages for insects and seeds, and also eats berries. Its habitat is undergrowth—tangles and thickets—which makes it hard to spot. But you may hear the Eastern Towhee rummaging around. It makes its cup-shaped nest of bark, twigs, and leaves and lines it with grasses and animal hair. Males have black backs, reddish sides, and a white belly. Females are similar to males, but they are brown instead of black.

>>> RANGE MAP

BREEDING

YEAR-ROUND

MIGRATION

WINTER

FEMALES ARE BROWN WITH REDDISH SIDES

MALES HAVE A BLACK HOOD AND UNDERPARTS, WITH REDDISH SIDES

LONG TAIL

10s spotters

be a BIRD NERD!

EASTERN TOWHEES seem more than a little clueless when it comes to intruders. Brown-headed Cowbirds often remove a towhee's eggs from its nest and substitute their own eggs without the towhee realizing it. This happens to half of all Eastern Towhee nests in some areas!

Laugh Out Loud!

What do you call a bird during the winter?

Brrrd!

SPOTTED TOWHEE

Pipilo maculatus LENGTH 7.5 in (19 cm) • HABITAT Thickets, forest edges, fields, canyon bottoms • FOOD Mostly insects, some acorns, seeds, berries • VOICE Song is a simple trill of variable speed

MALE SPOTTED TOWHEES are serious singers! During breeding season, they spend 70 to 90 percent of their mornings singing, hoping to attract a mate. Spotted Towhees live in thickets and tangles and are hard to glimpse. They like lots of brushy cover with fallen leaves on the ground, where they hunt for insects to eat, including beetles, crickets, bees, and wasps. They also eat acorns, berries, and seeds.

>>> RANGE MAP

BREEDING

YEAR-ROUND

MIGRATION

WINTER

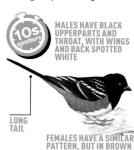

MALES HAVE BLACK UPPERPARTS AND THROAT, WITH WINGS AND BACK SPOTTED WHITE

LONG TAIL

FEMALES HAVE A SIMILAR PATTERN, BUT IN BROWN

CALIFORNIA TOWHEE

Melozone crissalis LENGTH 9 in (23 cm) • HABITAT Chaparral, parks, gardens • FOOD Seeds, insects, berries • VOICE Series of simple *chink* notes

MOSTLY BROWN with a little orange under its tail, the California Towhee generally stays close to where it nests. Pairs stay together all year and call back and forth—*chink chink chink*—as they scratch the ground hunting for insects and seeds. California Towhees often nest in poison oak, and the birds can eat the plant's berries without any bad effects.

>>> RANGE MAP

YEAR-ROUND

LONG TAIL

SHORT, ROUNDED WINGS

PLAIN BROWN WITH ORANGEY PATCH UNDER TAIL

CHIPPING SPARROW

Spizella passerina LENGTH 5.5 in (14 cm) • HABITAT Mix of trees and grassy openings • FOOD Insects, seeds • VOICE Song is a rapid trill of dry *chip* notes

THE CHIPPING SPARROW gets its name from its "chippy" call. Its colors are most vibrant in summer, when the bird wears a distinct reddish crown. At all times of the year, this sparrow shows a black line through the eye. A female Chipping Sparrow often builds a nest in a conifer at eye level. Some females line their nests with hair plucked from resting horses and sleeping dogs. Ouch!

NOTICEABLE REDDISH CROWN IN SPRING AND EARLY SUMMER

LONG TAIL

WINTER COLORS MORE SUBDUED

>>> RANGE MAP

BREEDING
YEAR-ROUND
MIGRATION
WINTER

SONG SPARROW

Melospiza melodia LENGTH 6 in (15 cm) • HABITAT Farmlands, brushy areas, backyards • FOOD Seeds, fruits, insects • VOICE Loud, musical song ends in trill

SONG SPARROWS don't have that name for nothing. One male followed by an observer sang more than 2,300 songs in one day! These sparrows vary in size and intensity of color depending on location. But all are reddish and gray with bold streaks on the breast that may form a central spot. They often perch on low shrubs. Listen for their trill.

ROUND HEAD IS REDDISH BROWN AND GRAY

SHORT, STOUT BILL

STREAKED SIDES

BREAST STREAKS OFTEN FORM SPOT

>>> RANGE MAP

BREEDING
YEAR-ROUND
WINTER

WHITE-THROATED SPARROW

Zonotrichia albicollis LENGTH 6.75 in (17 cm) ∙ HABITAT Brush, woodland edges ∙ FOOD Seeds, insects ∙ VOICE Song a thin whistle: *Old Sam Peabody, Peabody, Peabody*

YOU MIGHT SAY the White-throated Sparrow is the bird version of a chipmunk: It has a distinctive striped head and it eats seeds off the ground. In the spring, White-throated Sparrows travel north to breed, but in winter they stay in backyards and around forest edges. Attract them by scattering seeds.

>>> RANGE MAP

BREEDING
YEAR-ROUND
MIGRATION
WINTER

YELLOW SPOT BETWEEN THE EYE AND BILL

WHITE THROAT

BROWN ABOVE AND GRAY BELOW WITH BLACK-AND-WHITE-STRIPED HEAD

10s spotters

WHITE-CROWNED SPARROW

Zonotrichia leucophrys LENGTH 7 in (18 cm) ∙ HABITAT Brush, grasslands, woodland edges ∙ FOOD Seeds, insects ∙ VOICE Calls include a loud, metallic *pink*

EASY TO IDENTIFY, the White-crowned Sparrow shows up in the eastern United States in winter, but is much more common in the West, where some live year-round. These birds have distinctive crowns with thick, black and white stripes. Depending on location, the bill can be pink, orange, or yellow. White-crowns feed mostly on the ground, gleaning the seeds of weeds and grasses.

BLACK AND WHITE STRIPES ON THE HEAD

BACK STRIPED WITH BROWN AND PALE GRAYISH BROWN EDGES

LONG TAIL

10s spotters

>>> RANGE MAP

BREEDING
YEAR-ROUND
MIGRATION
WINTER

DARK-EYED JUNCO

Junco hyemalis **LENGTH 6.25 in (16 cm)** • **HABITAT Coniferous and deciduous forests, open woodlands, fields, parks, gardens** • **FOOD Seeds, insects** • **VOICE A sharp *dit* and rapid twittering**

ONE OF THE MOST common birds in North America, the Dark-eyed Junco can be found from California to Newfoundland and from Alaska to Mexico. One estimate puts the population at 630 million—twice the number of people living in the United States! Juncos have different looks in different locations. Eastern birds are mostly gray and white (Slate-colored Junco). Many western birds have a black or gray hood and rusty back (Oregon Junco). Other variations are found in the Central Plains and Rockies. All have white outer tail feathers. Dark-eyed Juncos breed in coniferous and deciduous forests. In winter they form huge flocks that hang out on the ground.

>>> RANGE MAP

BREEDING

YEAR-ROUND

WINTER

SLATE-COLORED IN FLIGHT

DARK GRAY OR BROWN ABOVE AND PALE BELOW

PINK BILL

ALL HAVE WHITE OUTER TAIL FEATHERS

"OREGON" FEMALE AND MALE

10s spotters

be a BIRD NERD!

When **DARK-EYED JUNCOS** fly away, look for their white outer tail feathers, which are very easy to see. A large amount of white in a male's tail may signal a well-fed bird—and a good potential mate!

TRY THiS!

Got a 2-liter soda bottle and two wooden spoons? You've got a bird feeder!

STEP 1: Remove wrapper, wash bottle, and let dry.

STEP 2: Mark an X about 2 inches (5 cm) from bottom; mark another one opposite.

STEP 3: Turn bottle a quarter turn and make same kinds of marks 3 inches (7.5 cm) higher.

STEP 4: With adult help, cut plastic at X marks so you can slide in the spoons by their handles (future perches).

STEP 5: Use a funnel to fill feeder with birdseed.

BIRDTASTICS: Chaparral Birds

Black-chinned Sparrow

Spizella atrogularis
LENGTH: 5.75 in (15 cm)
EATS: Seeds, insects
VOICE: Call is a high, thin *seep*

Wrentit

Chamaea fasciata
LENGTH: 6.5 in (17 cm)
EATS: Insects, spiders, fruits, seeds
VOICE: Call is a rattling *churr*

CHAPARRAL is a shrub-covered habitat that has hot, dry summers and mild or cool winters. Think of the cowboy country shown in movies and on television. It also has some woodland, like scrub oak, and floors layered with leaves and needles—perfect cover for escaping predators. Here the California Quail, Wrentit, and Black-chinned Sparrow find plenty of food, such as insects, spiders, and seeds.